9/19 5x

D0862612

COMPLETE STEP-BY-STEP GUIDE TO
Cake Decorating

WITHDRAWN
From Toronto Public Library

COMPLETE STEP-BY-STEP GUIDE TO
Cake Decorating

40 Stunning Cakes for All Occasions

CAROL DEACON

IMM **lifestyle books**™

Read. Learn. Do What You Love.

Published 2018—IMM Lifestyle Books
www.IMMLifestyleBooks.com

IMM Lifestyle Books are distributed in the UK by Grantham Book Service, Trent Road, Grantham, Lincolnshire, NG31 7XQ.

In North America, IMM Lifestyle Books are distributed by Fox Chapel Publishing, 903 Square Street, Mount Joy, PA 17552, *www.FoxChapelPublishing.com*.

© 2018 by IMM Lifestyle Books

Produced under license.

The patterns contained herein are copyrighted by the author. Readers may make copies of these patterns for personal use. The patterns themselves, however, are not to be duplicated for resale or distribution under any circumstances. Any such copying is a violation of copyright law.

ISBN 978-1-5048-0094-5

Library of Congress Cataloging-in-Publication Data

Names: Deacon, Carol, author.
Title: Complete step-by-step guide to cake decorating / Carol Deacon.
Description: Mount Joy, Pa. : IMM Lifestyle Books, [2018] | Includes index.
Identifiers: LCCN 2017050069 | ISBN 9781504800945
Subjects: LCSH: Cake decorating. | LCGFT: Cookbooks.
Classification: LCC TX771.2 .D426963 2018 | DDC 641.86/539--dc23
LC record available at https://lccn.loc.gov/2017050069

We are always looking for talented authors. To submit an idea, please send a brief inquiry to acquisitions@foxchapelpublishing.com.

Printed in Singapore
10 9 8 7 6 5 4 3 2 1

Shutterstock photos: Amawasri Pakdara (2, 7); Phonlamai Photo (6); Hrynevich Yury (21)

• •

In memory of Malcolm Martin Deacon
who loved fishing, cricket…
and cake!

• •

NOTES

Every effort has been made to present clear and accurate instructions. Therefore, the author and publisher can offer no guarantee or accept any liability for any injury, illness, or damage, which may inadvertently be caused to the user while following these instructions.

Because of the slight risk of salmonella, raw eggs should not be served to the very young, the ill, the elderly, or to pregnant women.

In the recipes, use either metric or imperial measurements, but never a combination of the two, since exact conversions are not always possible.

ACKNOWLEDGMENTS

Carol Deacon would like to thank Pamela Eve, Elyane, Paul, Stephen, Rosie, and Holly Jones and Juliette and Charlie for their help "Twiggy sitting" during the making of this book. Carol would also like to thank Valerie Hedgethorne for her marzipan recipe on page 100.

Contents

Introduction

Probably the most commonly uttered phrase when a decorated cake is brought out at a special occasion is "Oh, isn't that lovely, . . ." quickly followed by "I could never do that!" Well, guess what? Neither could I, once.

The secret behind successful cake decorating is not having a steady hand, and eye for color, a creative mother, or any of the other excuses that I've heard over the years. In fact, there are really only two secrets to cake decorating. The first is to just jump in and give it a try, and the second is to allow yourself enough time.

However, just taking yourself to the home baking aisle in your supermarket or into the nearest cake decorating supply store with no real idea of what to buy will result in bewilderment, frustration, and quite possibly, an empty space on the table where a cake should have been. So here's how the *Complete Step-by-Step Guide to Cake Decorating* can help you.

From baking the perfect sponge cake to icing a wedding cake, I have explained and demystified many of the techniques used to create simple but stunning cakes. This is not the most technical cake book on the market, but that's because I have tried to take the simplest route to a great end result without scaring anyone.

Primarily this book is aimed at the beginners or those with a little experience who want to take their skills further. However, because some of the ideas are so simple and quick, it will also appeal to those with years of experience, too. After all, you may be the most experienced cake decorator in the world, but I bet you still get asked to produce things at the last minute!

It is easy to forget that cooking, especially preparing special items like these, is not knowledge that any of us is born with. It involves reading, learning, and practicing. However, I believe that learning should be enjoyable, information understandable, and great results easily attainable.

So, now you are about to learn a lot of new things that you never knew you wanted to know. But best of all, you are about to bring joy to a lot of people. Just watch their faces light up when you bring out your creation. I bet if you listen carefully, you'll hear the odd whisper of "Oh, isn't that lovely, . . . I could never do that!"

Easter Cake (see pages 148-9)

BAKING BASICS

This section gives you all of the basic information that you need to know before you actually start making the cake. There is advice on what you need to think about before you start, cake sizes and portions, information on baking pans and how to line them, and a fail-safe way of calculating how much mixture you need. Basically, you'll find everything you need to know to get you started.

There are certain questions that you need to think about beforehand to ensure that the finished cake is everything that you wanted it to be:
· How many people will the cake need to serve?
· What sort of cake does/do the recipient/s like?
· What style of cake is needed?
· How much time do you have?
· Are there things you can do in advance?

Cake sizes and portions

To get the maximum number of portions out of a cake, it is best to cut it into fingers rather than wedges.

To give you an idea of the size of cake you should be baking, opposite is a guide to the approximate number of portions you can get from cakes of various sizes.

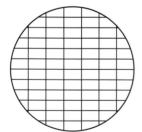 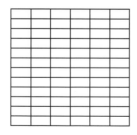

Above: These diagrams show the best way to cut a round and a square cake.

SIZE AND PORTION GUIDE		
Size	Sponge Cake	Fruit Cake
6 in. (15cm) round	10	20
6 in. (15cm) square	15	25
7 in. (18cm) round	15	30
7 in. (18cm) square	20	40
8 in. (20cm) round	20	40
8 in. (20cm) square	25	50
9 in. (23cm) round	25	50
9 in. (23cm) square	35	70
10 in. (25cm) round	30	65
10 in. (25cm) square	45	90
11 in. (28cm) round	40	85
11 in. (28cm) square	55	110
12 in. (30cm) round	50	100
12 in. (30cm) square	65	130

Cutting cakes

To be sure you have enough to feed everyone, a cutting cake can be made. This cake does not have any decoration on it. It should be made to match the main cake—fruitcake, sponge cake, chocolate cake, or whatever and covered with the same kind of icing, but it is then left plain, as it will never be on show. It is especially useful at weddings to have a spare cake like this to provide lots of extra slices.

Baking pans

There are all kinds pans available for baking cakes. Some are rigid all-in-one pans; others have a spring-release mechanism that releases the sides of the pan, freeing the cake; while even more others have a separate top and side section that allows you to push the cake out of the pan when baked. There is also an increasing variety of shaped pans available, from numbers and letters, hearts and stars, to cartoon characters. There is no hard and fast rule as to what type of pan (spring-release, rigid, and so on) is best for a particular cake. You just need to ensure that whatever size or shape of pan you use, that it will provide you with enough cake for your chosen design.

Lining a cake pan

Lining a cake pan sometimes seems like the most tedious part of the whole cake-making process, but it really is the only way to ensure that all of your cake comes out of the pan in one piece. There are several products on the market, such as "cooking sprays" that claim that if you use them, there is no need to line your pan. I can't comment on whether they are effective or not since I've never used them. Regardless, I prefer to line my pans.

Some specialty or online suppliers sell precut paper cake pan liners, which you simply put in the pan eliminating the need to add grease of any kind. I have used one of those in the Monster Cupcake on pages 156–7, where it even becomes part of the finished creation.

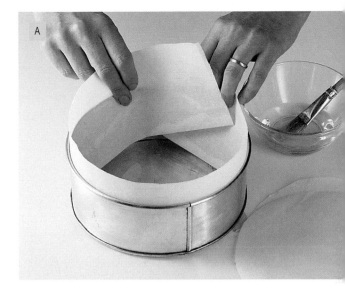

A

You can use either waxed paper or parchment paper to line the pan. The only difference is that the parchment paper does not need to be greased. The following directions will walk you through the correct way to line a cake pan.

1. Measure the circumference and height of the pan. Cut out a strip of waxed paper or parchment paper to that length and about 1 in. (2cm) wider than the height of the pan.

2. Place the pan on another piece of paper and draw around the base. Cut out the drawn shape.

3. Wipe a little butter or margarine around the inside of the pan.

4. Place the long strip around the inside of the pan (Fig. a). Slip the other piece into the bottom of the pan.

B

Lining a cake pan for fruitcake

The method for lining a pan ready for baking a fruitcake is exactly the same as for a sponge cake, except that you need to double-line the pan. This will protect the sides and base of the cake during its long cooking time. So cut out two strips for the sides and two base pieces.

It is also advisable to wrap a double layer of parchment paper or waxed paper around the outside of the pan. Tie string around the outside to hold it in place (Fig. b).

How to calculate how much mixture is needed for an unusually shaped pan

Not all cake pans are square or round. Here's a handy tip to work out how much cake mixture you will need.

1. Fill a cup with water. Tip the water into the pan. Repeat until the water has reached the level that the unbaked cake mixture would reach if the pan were filled—this is usually about 1 in. (2.5cm) from the top. Count how many cups get filled.

2. Now take a cake pan for which you know how much cake mixture would be needed; for instance, an 8 in. (20cm) round pan that would take a four-egg sponge cake mixture. Using the same cup, count how many cups of water would be needed to fill that pan.

3. If the number of cups to fill the unusually shaped pan is double the cups required to fill the 8 in. (20cm) round pan, then you know that you need to make double the quantity of cake mixture. If it is half, then you know you need to make half and so on.

CAKE RECIPES

In the rush to get to the exciting, decorating part, it is easy to overlook the baking. However, no matter how exotic a cake looks, a cake is made to be eaten and it absolutely has to taste as good as it looks. Here are some basic cake recipes; they are my reliable favorites, and they always taste great.

INGREDIENTS				
Square pan	—	6 in. (15 cm)	7 in. (18 cm)	8 in. (20 cm)
Round pan	6 in. (15 cm)	7 in. (18 cm)	8 in. (20 cm)	9 in. (23 cm)
Self-rising flour	¾ cup 6 oz. (175 g)	1 cup 8 oz. (225 g)	1¼ cup 10 oz. (285 g)	1½ cup 12 oz. (350 g)
Super fine (Caster) sugar	½ cup 4 oz. (115 g)	¾ cup 6 oz. (170 g)	1 cup 8 oz. (230 g)	1¼ cup 10 oz. (285 g)
Butter (softened)	½ cup 4 oz. (115 g)	¾ cup 6 oz. (170 g)	1 cup 8 oz. (230 g)	1¼ cup 10 oz. (285 g)
Eggs (large)	2	3	4	5
Milk	1 tbsp. (15 ml)	1 tbsp. (15 ml)	2 tbsp. (30 ml)	3 tbsp. (45 ml)
Baking time (approx.)	1¼–1½ hrs	1¼–1½ hrs	1½–1¾ hrs	1½–2 hrs

Madeira sponge cake

This sponge cake recipe is extremely easy to make. You just put all the ingredients in a bowl and mix. An electric mixer makes light work of the mixing and takes only a minute. It will take longer if you're mixing by hand. To make things easier for yourself, make sure the butter is very soft.

1. Grease and line the relevant cake pan (see pages 11–2) and preheat your oven to 300°F/150°C/Gas mark 2. (Timings and temperatures for conventional ovens may vary. Refer to your manufacturer's handbook for guidance.)

2. Sift the flour into a mixing bowl to get some air into it and add the rest of the ingredients.

3. Set the mixer to a slow setting, and slowly combine all ingredients together.

4. Increase the speed and beat for a minute until the mixture becomes pale and silky.

5. Spoon the mixture into a prepared pan and smooth the top.

6. Bake for the required time. When ready, the cake should have pulled away slightly from the edges of the pan. If pressed lightly, the top should spring back from the touch. Insert a sharp knife or cake skewer into the cake. If it comes out clean, the cake is ready.

7. Turn the cake upside down on a cooling rack. Remove the lining and let cool.

Storing: Ice the cake when cool or cover in plastic wrap until ready. Use and eat within five days.
Freezing: Once baked and cooled, this sponge cake can be frozen for up to three months.

Flavor variations

Chocolate Add a tablespoon of cocoa powder in place of a tablespoon of flour for a quick chocolate sponge cake.

Orange/lemon For a hint of citrus, add the grated zest of an orange or lemon before baking.

Almond Add a teaspoon of almond extract to the basic mixture.

Coconut Add 2 oz. (60g) shredded coconut to the mixture.

Glass bowl cakes, layer cakes, and mini-cupcakes

Use the three-egg sponge cake mixture to make a 1 qt. (1 L) glass bowl cake for the Monster Cupcake (see pages 156–7), 24 mini-cupcakes cakes for the Fearsome Dragon (see pages 86–7), or two layer cakes for the Quick Chocolate Cake (see pages 144–5).

Make sure the glass bowl is heatproof and oven-safe. Grease the inside and place a disk of waxed paper in the base. After removing the cake from the oven, slide a palette knife around the edge of the bowl to release it. Tip onto a cooling rack and peel off the waxed paper disk. If you don't have a bowl, bake a square cake and carve it into a rounded shape.

Mini-cupcakes are fun, easy to make, and can be decorated in many different ways.

Chocolate cake

This cake takes a little more effort than the simple chocolate sponge cake recipe on pages 13–4, but the velvet texture of the finished cake makes the effort worthwhile. A crust will form on the top of the cake as it bakes; it might even scorch slightly. Don't worry, this is normal and will not affect the taste of the cake underneath. Slice the crust off the cake after it has cooled and just before decorating.

1. Grease and line the relevant cake pan (see pages 11–2) and preheat the oven to 350°F/180°C/Gas mark 4. (Timings and temperatures for conventional ovens may vary. Refer to your manufacturer's handbook for guidance.)

2. Separate the egg whites from the yolks and set aside in two small bowls.

3. Melt the chocolate in a heatproof bowl (see page 136).

4. In a mixing bowl, cream the softened butter and superfine sugar together.

5. Beat in the egg yolks and then the melted chocolate.

6. Set the mixer to a low speed and slowly stir in the flour. Stop as soon as it has all been incorporated. Set aside.

7. Put the egg whites into a second mixing bowl. Connect the whisk attachment to your mixer and whisk the egg whites until stiff. Whisk in the confectioners' sugar.

8. Reattach the beater to the mixer and slowly stir the chocolate mixture into the egg whites.

9. Pour into the prepared pan and bake immediately. The crust on top of the cake can make it difficult to tell if the cake is done baking by touch alone so carefully cut a little section of crust away from the center of the cake. Insert a knife or cake skewer. If it comes out clean, the cake is ready.

10. Turn the cake out onto a cooling rack. Remove the paper lining and let cool.

Storing: Frost the cake within a day of baking. If this is not possible, freeze until required.
Freezing: When cooled, this cake will freeze well for up to three months. Leave the crust on if freezing.

INGREDIENTS				
Square pan	—	6 in. (15 cm)	7 in. (18 cm)	8 in. (20 cm)
Round pan	6 in. (15 cm)	7 in. (18 cm)	8 in. (20 cm)	9 in. (23 cm)
Butter (softened)	¼ cup 3 oz. (90 g)	½ cup 4 oz. (115 g)	¾ cup 6 oz. (170 g)	1 cup 8 oz. (230 g)
Superfine (Caster) sugar	2½ tbsp. 1¼ oz. (40 g)	¼ cup 2½ oz. (75 g)	½ cup 4 oz. (115 g)	¾ cup 5 oz. (150 g)
Eggs (large)	3	4	6	8
Semisweet chocolate	¾ cup 5 oz. (150 g)	¾ cup 6 oz. (170 g)	1 cup 8 oz. (230 g)	1¼ cup 10 oz. (285 g)
Self-rising flour	¼ cup 3 oz. (90 g)	½ cup 4 oz. (115 g)	¾ cup 6 oz. (170 g)	1 cup 8 oz. (230 g)
Confetioners' sugar	2 tbsp. 1 oz. (30 g)	2 tbsp. 1 oz. (30 g)	4 tbsp. 2 oz. (60 g)	¼ cup 3 oz. (90 g)
Baking time (approx.)	45–55 mins	45 mins– 1 hr	1–1¼ hrs	1–1¼ hrs

Quick Chocolate Cake (see pages 144-5)

Special effects with sponge cake

Forget decorating for a moment; there are a few special effects that can be achieved with the cake itself.

Checkered sponge cake

This effect is fun, as from the outside it looks like an ordinary cake, but when you cut into it you have a checkered effect. You need two round sponge cakes of contrasting colors; usually a plain sponge cake and a chocolate sponge cake are used.

1. Using cutters, cut two rounds out of the plain sponge cake. Do the same with the chocolate cake (Fig. a).

2. Before assembling the cake, coat the inside of each piece with buttercream or jam. Swap the middles around—so the middle of the chocolate cake goes into the middle of the plain sponge cake and vice versa (Fig. b).

3. Sandwich the cakes together with your chosen filling (Fig. c).

Striped sponge cake

This is another way of adding interest to the cake itself. Children especially like the surprise of seeing the unexpected when the cake is cut. You need two round sponge cakes of contrasting colors; usually a plain sponge cake and a chocolate sponge cake are used.

1. Cut each cake in half. Reassemble the cake by sandwiching together the plain and chocolate sponge cake pieces in alternate layers (Fig. d).

2. You can use your filling of choice to assemble the layers. Try to keep the layers as level as possible (Fig. e).

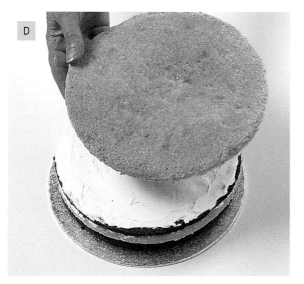

D

E

Fruitcake

I've said this before, but I'll say it again since it's so true—there is absolutely nothing that beats the seasonal aroma of cinnamon and spices wafting through the house in the dreary winter months before Christmas. Visitors to your home will not only want to stir the mixture and make a wish but they will also start telling you tales of how they used to visit their grandmothers when they were young, and how she used to bake wonderful cakes. Before you know it, you will have spread the Christmas spirit without even trying.

Making your own fruitcake is a lot easier than you might think. The secret is to make sure you have everything together before you start. See Substitutions on page 165 for hard-to-find ingredients.

1. Place all the dried fruit into a bowl and pour the brandy over them. Stir and cover the bowl with a plate. Let the fruit soak for a few hours, preferably overnight.

2. Prepare the cake pan (see pages 11–2) and preheat the oven to 300°F/150°C/Gas mark 2. (Timings and temperatures for conventional ovens may vary. Refer to your manufacturer's handbook for guidance.)

3. Cream the butter and sugar together, then beat in the eggs.

4. Sift the flour. Slowly mix in the sifted flour, spices, and ground almonds. Add a little more flour if it seems too runny.

5. Stir in the soaked fruit, lemon zest, and flaked almonds. Spoon the mixture into the prepared pan. Smooth the surface and bake.

INGREDIENTS				
Currants	5 oz. (150g)	6 oz. (175g)	7 oz. (200g)	8 oz. (225g)
Black raisins	5 oz. (150g)	6 oz. (175g)	7 oz. (200g)	8 oz. (225g)
Golden raisins	5 oz. (150g)	6 oz. (175g)	7 oz. (200g)	8 oz. (225g)
Candied fruit peel	1 oz. (30g)	1½oz. (45g)	2 oz. (60g)	2½oz. (75g)
Candied cherries	2 oz. (60g)	2½oz. (75g)	3 oz. (90g)	3½oz. (100g)
Brandy	4 tbsp. (60ml)	6 tbsp. (90ml)	8 tbsp. (120ml)	8 tbsp. (120ml)
Butter (softened)	5 oz. (150g)	6 oz. (175g)	7 oz. (200g)	8 oz. (225g)
Dark brown sugar	5 oz. (150g)	6 oz. (175g)	7 oz. (200g)	8 oz. (225g)
Eggs (large)	3	4	5	6
All-purpose flour	6 oz. (175g)	7 oz. (200g)	8 oz. (225g)	9 oz. (270g)
Mixed spice	2 tsp.	2 tsp.	1 tbsp.	1 tbsp.
Ground cinnamon	½ tsp.	½ tsp.	¾ tsp.	1 tsp.
Ground almonds	¾oz. (20g)	1 oz. (30g)	1½oz. (45g)	2 oz. (60g)
Flaked almonds	¾oz. (20g)	1 oz. (30g)	1½oz. (45g)	2 oz. (60g)
Lemon (zest only)	½	½	1	1
Square pan	6 in. (15cm)	7 in. (18cm)	8 in. (20cm)	9 in. (23cm)
Round pan	7 in. (18cm)	8 in. (20cm)	9 in. (23cm)	10 in. (25cm)
Baking time (approx.)	1½–2 hrs	1¾–2¼ hrs	2–2¼ hrs	2¼–2¾ hrs

6. Check the cake 15 to 20 minutes before the end of the baking time. If the top is turning very brown, place a disk of parchment paper over the top.

7. To test the cake, insert a sharp knife or cake skewer. If it comes out clean, the cake is done.

8. Allow the cake to cool completely in the pan. If you will be using the cake right away, turn it upside down when cooled and remove the paper lining.

Storing: You can store this cake for up to three months. When cooled, tip it out of the baking pan, leaving the paper around the sides. Poke a few holes in the top of the cake with a toothpick and drizzle some brandy over the top. Let the brandy soak in and then wrap the cake in two sheets of waxed paper. Double-wrap it again using two sheets of aluminum foil and place in a box or cabinet until required. Do not store it in a plastic airtight container since this can encourage mold growth. You can "feed" your cake every one to two weeks with a little more brandy if you wish.
Freezing: If you plan to keep the cake longer than three months, wrap it in waxed paper and freeze until required. Defrost thoroughly for about 8 hours at room temperature before serving.

Microwave cakes
In case of a dessert emergency, here are a couple of cakes you can cook in four minutes! The texture is slightly different from that of oven-baked cakes, and the vanilla cake will look pale since it will not brown on top. Be sure to never use a metal cake pan in a microwave oven.

Vanilla cake
This recipe is for a 7 in. (18cm) round microwaveable cake dish.
INGREDIENTS
- ½ cup (125g/4 oz.) butter
- ½ cup (113g/4 oz.) superfine (caster) sugar
- 2 eggs
- 1 tsp. vanilla extract
- 1 cup (128g/4½ oz.) self-rising flour
- ½ tsp. baking powder

1. Grease the microwaveable dish and place a disk of waxed paper in the base.

2. Cream the butter and sugar together until fluffy. Beat in the eggs and vanilla extract. Fold in the flour and baking powder.

3. Spoon into the prepared dish and bake on full power for 4 minutes (or until a toothpick inserted in the center of the cake comes out clean).

4. Let the cake stand for 10 minutes before turning it onto a cooling rack.

Chocolate cake
This recipe is for a 7 in. (18cm) round microwaveable cake dish.
INGREDIENTS
- ½ cup (125g/4 oz.) butter
- ½ cup (113g/4 oz.) granulated sugar
- 2 eggs
- ¾ cup (96g/3 oz.) self-rising flour
- ¼ cup (30g/1 oz.) cocoa powder
- 1 tsp. baking powder

TROUBLESHOOTING

We all want our cakes to turn out perfectly every time, but sometimes they don't, even if you're an experienced cook. Here are some of the most common problems and advice on how to avoid them.

Problem: The cake sank in the center.
Possible reasons:
· The mixture was too runny.
· The oven door was opened too soon and for too long during the cooking process.
· The oven wasn't hot enough.
· The cake was not cooked long enough.

Problem: The cake burned.
Possible reasons:
· The cake was placed too near the top of the oven. Always cook in the center of the oven, even with conventional ovens.
· The oven was too hot. No matter what it says on the temperature dial, ovens do vary. Next time, cook it on a slightly lower heat setting.

Problem: The cake seemed very dry.
Possible reasons:
· It was overcooked. Reduce the cooking time the next time you make it.
· There wasn't enough liquid in the mixture. If it's virtually impossible to stir the uncooked cake mixture, you need to add a little more milk or egg.

Problem: The fruit sank.
Possible reasons:
· The oven door was opened for too long during cooking.
· There was too much flour in the mixture.

1. Grease the microwaveable dish and place a disk of waxed paper in the base.

2. Cream the butter and sugar together until fluffy.

3. Beat in the eggs. Stir in the flour, cocoa, and baking powder.

4. Cook on full power for 4 minutes (or until a toothpick inserted in the center comes out clean).

5. Let the cake stand for 10 minutes before turning it onto a cooling rack.

NUMBER AND LETTER CAKES

Thinking of new decorating ideas for birthday cakes year after year can be quite difficult. Creating number and letter shapes out of round or square cakes is very simple to do. The recipient will always appreciate the finished cake because it is very personal to them.

Numbers

The easiest way to bake a cake in the shape of a number is to buy a cake pan in the shape of the required number (Fig. a). To work out how much cake mixture you will need, use the tip given on page 12 for calculating the amount required to fill an unusually shaped pan.

Grease the sides of the pan and line it with a strip of waxed paper. If the pan has a base, trace around the pan itself and cut out a piece to lay on the base of the pan. Stand the pan on a baking sheet while cooking so the heat is evenly distributed along the base of the cake.

If you cannot obtain a number shaped pan, you can cut numbers out of square and round cakes instead (Fig. b). On page 26 you will find a guide to show you how you can cut any number out of round and square cakes.

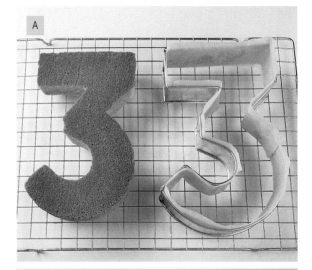

A

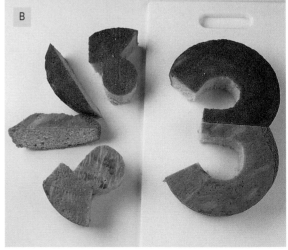

B

Left: A simple option is to decorate the cake with candy arranged in a number on the top.

One way to deal with "holes" in letters or numbers is
to ignore them and to place a toy figure or candles
in the spot where a "hole" would normally be.

Guide to cutting numbers out of square and round cakes.

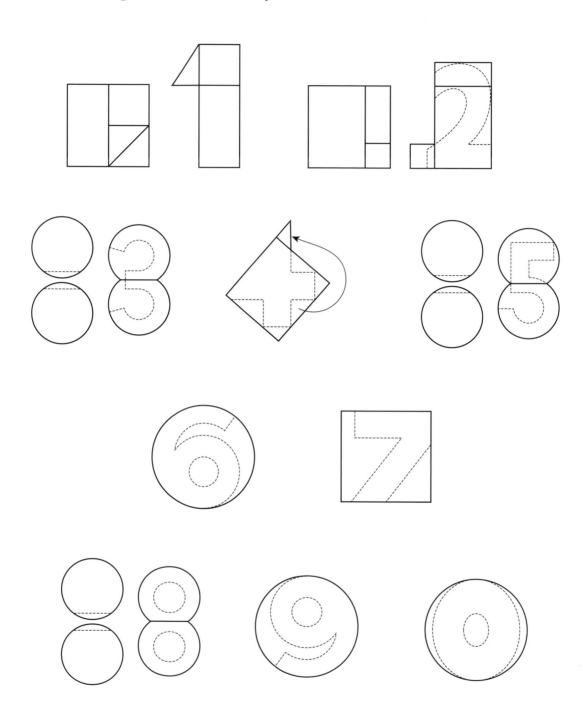

Decorating number-shaped cakes with buttercream frosting

The easiest way to decorate an irregularly shaped cake is to cover it with buttercream frosting.

1. Slice the cake into layers as you would a round or square cake.

2. Reassemble it, filling the layers with frosting. Place on a cake board.

3. Spread frosting around the sides and top (Fig. a) and decorate with candies or other decorations of your choice.

Numbers with holes

To decorate a cake in the shape of a number with a hole in it, such as a six, you will need to use a slightly different method.

1. Cut the cake into the desired shape and then slice into layers.

2. Cut a hole out of the top layer only.

3. Spread a little black buttercream frosting in the center of the next layer. Don't go right to the edge or the black frosting will "leak" out of the sides when you reassemble the cake.

4. Spread your chosen color of frosting around the outside of the black frosting on the lower layer and around the outside of the hole in the top layer (Fig. b).

5. Reassemble the cake and spread frosting around the sides and top of the cake. Pipe frosting or arrange candies around the edges of the cake.

Decorating with fondant

Simple rounded or straight numbers like 0 or 1 can normally be covered all at one time. Numbers with a lot of curved edges and corners like a 3 will take more time.

1. Slice and fill the cake with buttercream frosting and place it in position on the cake board. Spread a thin coating of frosting around the outside of the cake. This will ensure that the fondant sticks to the cake.

2. Roll out the fondant. Using the baking pan as a template, cut out an outline of the number and place it on top of the cake. Paint a light line of water around the cut edge of the fondant topping.

3. Roll out some more fondant and cut out a long, thin strip. The width of the strip should be the same measurement as the height of the cake, including the fondant topping.

4. Roll up the strip like a loose bandage and unroll it around the sides of the cake (Fig. c). To hide the joins, either pipe or crimp along the top edge of the cake (see page 80).

Letters

The same decorating techniques that were used for covering numbers can also be used to decorate letter-shaped cakes. If you are unable to find a cake pan with your desired letter, you can create your own out of round or square cakes. You can use any leftover pieces of cake to make delicious truffles (see page 141).

"T" is a very simple shape to cut out of a square cake.

Guide for cutting letters out of square and round cakes

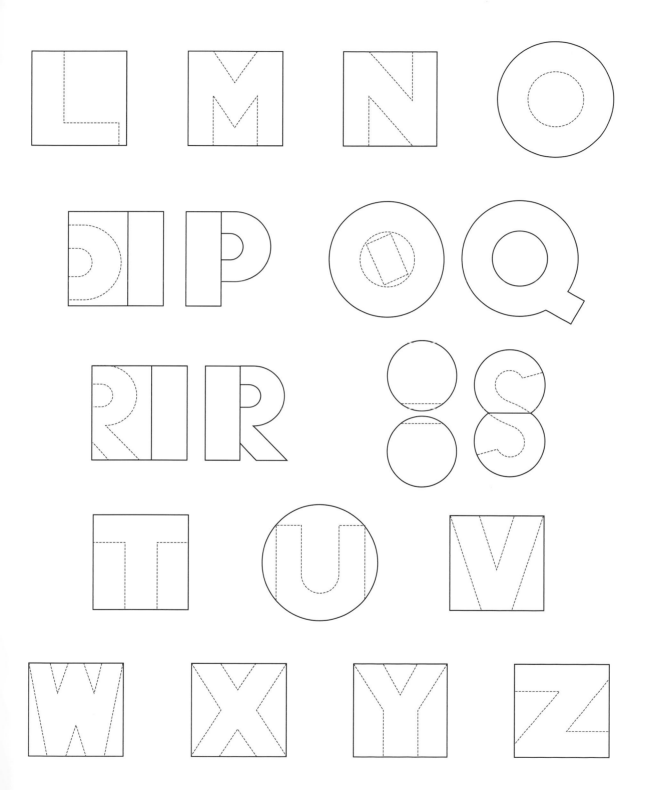

BASIC EQUIPMENT

It is not necessary to purchase everything listed here before you can decorate your first cake. A carving knife, rolling pin, small sharp knife, palette knife, and a paintbrush are the barest essentials. If you enjoy using fondant, it would be worth buying a cake smoother, since using one dramatically improves the finish of the cake. Build up your collection gradually. A plastic toolbox, which you can buy inexpensively from a local hardware store, is an ideal container for your tools.

Turntable (1) Although not, strictly speaking, essential, once you've used one, you'll wonder what you ever did without it. Cheaper versions are available in plastic.

Ruler (2) Not just for measuring; a ruler can also be useful for pressing lines and patterns into fondant.

Measuring spoons (3) A standard set ensures that you use the same quantities each time you make a recipe.

Scissors (4) A decent pair of sharp scissors is essential for making piping bags, cutting linings for pans and, sometimes, fondant.

Tape measure (5) Useful for measuring cakes and cake boards to ensure you have rolled out enough fondant.

Piping nozzles or tips (6) A varied selection is always useful, and they can double as small circle cutters. Metal nozzles are more expensive than plastic but are sharper and more accurate.

Small dishes (7) These are useful for holding water when modeling or for holding confectioners' sugar when rolling out fondant. Also, they're ideal when mixing food coloring into icing.

Baking pans (8) An assortment of shapes and sizes is useful.

Strainer/sifter (9) This item is vital for sifting flour and confectioners' sugar. It's also a useful tool for making bushes or hair by simply pushing a lump of fondant through the mesh.

Drinking straws (10) These can be used as tiny circle cutters and are ideal for making eyes. Held at

an angle and pressed into fondant, they can also be used for making the scales on snakes, dinosaurs, and so on.

Toothpicks (11) Use these for adding food coloring to fondant and for making frills and dotted patterns.

Rolling pin (12) A long rolling pin like the one shown will not leave handle dents in the fondant. Tiny ones are also available and are useful for rolling out small quantities of fondant when modeling. If you don't have a small rolling pin, a paintbrush handle will often do the job just as well.

Cake smoother (13) By using a smoother like an iron and running it over the surface of a covered cake, small bumps and lumps can literally be ironed out; essential for achieving a smooth finish.

Cutters (14) A vast range of shapes is available in both plastic and metal.

Cooling rack (15) Available in all shapes and sizes and used for cooling cakes.

Mixing bowl (16) Essential for mixing cake mixture. Useful for mixing food coloring into icing.

Small sharp knife (17) A small kitchen knife with a sharp, straight blade will become one of your most important pieces of equipment.

Cutting board (18) Essential for protecting work surfaces.

Paintbrushes (19) A medium brush is good for sticking things with water when modeling and cleaning out piping nozzles. A fine one is needed for adding delicate detail. Sable brushes are best.

Soft pastry brush (20) It is useful to have two brushes—one for dampening or cleaning

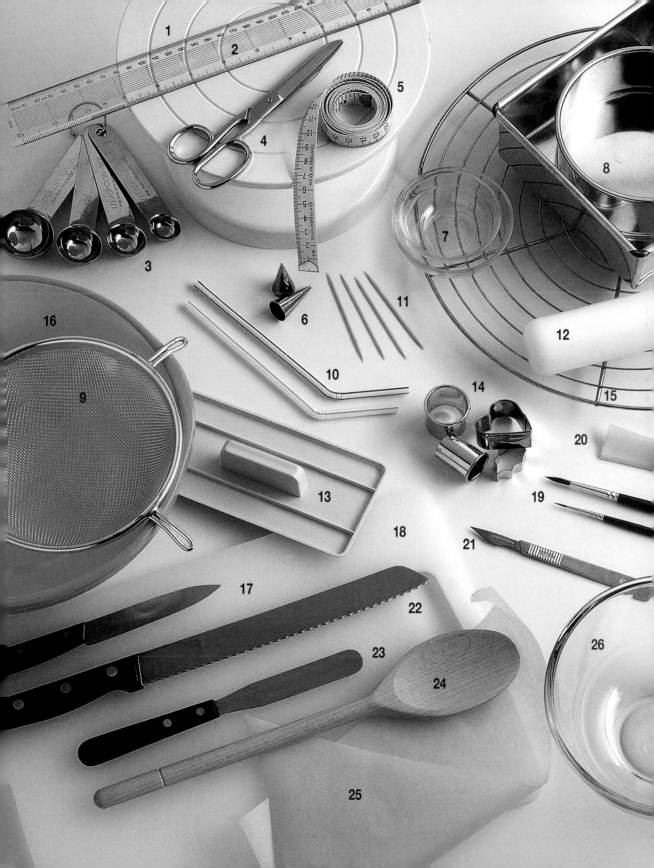

large areas, the other for brushing away dusty fingerprints or specks of dried fondant.

Scalpel (21) Invaluable when careful cutting is required, such as when scribing around a template.

Carving knife (22) A long, sharp serrated knife is essential for shaping and slicing cakes.

Palette knife (metal spatula) (23) Use this for spreading jam or buttercream frosting, mixing food coloring into larger quantities of royal icing, and lifting small pieces of fondant.

Wooden spoon (24) As well as for stirring cake mixture, the handle can be used as a modeling tool.

Waxed/ parchment paper (25) Used for lining pans, making piping bags, and storing fruitcakes. Can be used in place of tracing paper.

Glass bowl (26) Perfect for mixing food coloring into icing and baking rounded cakes, If using this bowl for baking, make sure it's oven-safe

Ribbons

A collection of ribbons is a must if you're going to take up cake decorating. They make fantastic instant decorations (see Christmas Bows on pages 122–3).

A ribbon is often placed around the edge of a cake board, particularly on cakes for special occasions. Double-sided tape is probably the best thing to use to secure the ribbon to the edge of the board since it will not bleed through the ribbon or taint the taste of the cake.

Instant decorations

Don't despair if you've left things to the last minute. Candy, candied fruit, flowers, store-bought decorations, and ribbon can all be used to make colorful instant decorations. Even a paper doily can be used to create an instant dramatic effect (see pages 144–5).

There are retail specialty stores and online sites (see Suppliers on page 165) that carry a wide variety of cake decorating items—some edible, some not. Your local supermarket is another good source, where you will find a range of decorations including sprinkles, nonpareils, and edible silver balls. Silk flowers are another great way of decorating a cake quickly (see page 88).

Candles

Try to make candles part of the design. Use colors that compliment the cake. On novelty cakes, it might be possible to stand them in thick, cut-out shapes or in balls of fondant so that they tie in with the design. You can even stick candles into marshmallows, then fix the marshmallows onto the cake board with dabs of royal icing or buttercream frosting. Be very careful if you're using candles on cakes that use edible decorating paper or silk flower decorations that are flammable. Position them well away from the decorations, light for the minimum amount of time, and never leave unattended.

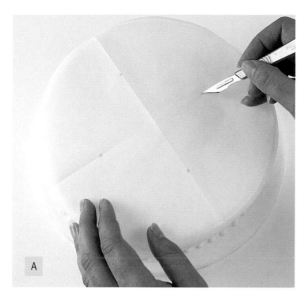

A

Pillars

There are many different styles and designs of pillars, some plain, some incredibly decorative. Although most of the cake designs in this book do not include pillars, here is a brief look at the basics of what they are and how to use them, in case you decide that you want to adapt one of the designs to include pillars.

Pillars have plastic dowels inside them, which are special plastic rods manufactured to comply with food regulations. They are available from specialty stores or online (see Suppliers on page 165). Although pillars might look sturdy, it is the hidden dowels that bear the weight of the cakes above.

Cake stands

Cake stands are an easy way of displaying wedding cakes and are a great idea for the beginner as well as the professional. There are many styles and designs available (see Suppliers on page 165). They can range from two tiers to six or more. A two-tier stand was used for the Wedding Star on pages 124–5.

Using pillars on fondant or buttercream frosted cakes

1. Decide how many pillars you want—usually three or four. Using waxed paper, make a template of the top of the cake by drawing around the pan it was baked in.

2. Fold the template in half and half again. Unfold the paper and make a mark on one of the folds—the distance in from the edge of the cake you'd like the pillar to be. Make corresponding marks on the other folds.

3. Place the template on top of the cake and using something like a pin or tip of a scalpel, make a tiny mark through each of the dots onto the surface of the cake (Fig. a). Remove the template.

4. Measure the height of the cake and the height of the pillar and add the two measurements together. Make a mark on one of the cake dowels the same length as that of the joint measurement.

5. Using a serrated knife, make a little saw mark at that point on the dowel and then bend and snap off the unwanted section.

6. Slot the dowel into one of the marked positions on the cake. Slide the pillar on top. Repeat for all of the other pillars (Fig. b on the next page). Because the pillars bear the weight of the cake above, it is essential that the top of the dowel be level with the top of the pillar. If it is lower, the pillar will be squashed down into the cake beneath.

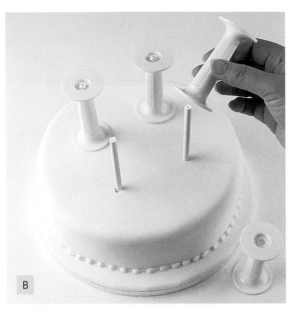

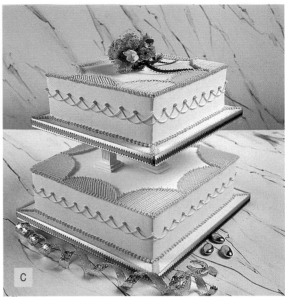

Using pillars on royal-iced cakes

There are various ways of using pillars on a traditional royal-iced fruitcake, but here is the simplest, quickest method. To prepare the cakes, cover each fruitcake with marzipan and a minimum of three thin coatings of royal icing. Allow each coating to dry thoroughly before applying the next. It is essential that the top of each iced cake be flat and level; use a small level to check. Fig. c shows a two-tier cake.

When the iced cake has dried, make marks on the cake's surface for the pillars. Scratch a hole into the icing at each of these points using the tip of a scalpel or scriber. The hole needs to be big enough to accommodate a cake dowel. Then follow steps 4 to 6 opposite under "Using pillars on fondant or buttercream frosted buttercream frosted cakes" on the previous page.

BUTTERCREAM FROSTING

Buttercream frosting is probably the easiest type of frosting to both make and use. Made from a mixture of butter, confectioners' sugar, and a little water, it can be used to fill and cover cakes and for piping and making decorations.

Recipe
Making up a batch of buttercream frosting will only take you a few minutes.

INGREDIENTS
(Amounts for 1 quantity)
- 1 cup (225g/8 oz.) softened butter, preferably unsalted
- 1 lb. 2 oz. (500g) confectioners' sugar
- 1 Tbsp. boiled, hot water
- 1 tsp. vanilla extract

1. Beat the butter until fluffy.

2. Add the sugar, water, and vanilla extract. Beat until pale and creamy.

Different flavors
White or milk chocolate
Stir either 3½ oz. (100g) of melted white or semisweet chocolate or 1 Tbsp. of cocoa powder mixed to a paste with about 1–2 Tbsp. of hot water into the frosting.

Coffee
Mix about 1 Tbsp. of instant coffee into 1 Tbsp. of water and beat into the frosting.

Various extracts
Instead of using vanilla extract, you can use peppermint, lemon, or almond extracts to flavor frosting. Just add a few drops and mix in.

Coloring buttercream
It is best to use paste food coloring since it is not as runny as the liquid coloring. You can liquid food coloring with buttercream frosting but because of its consistency, you will only be able to tint the frosting lightly. Add more confectioners' sugar if the frosting starts to get too thin and out of control.

Since buttercream frosting has a naturally creamy color, some colors like pale blue and pale pink will never be quite as true as they would be if you were adding the food coloring into pure white royal icing. However, if you beat and beat and beat buttercream frosting (and you'll need a mixer for this; otherwise, your arm will drop off!), it will eventually turn almost white and will take very pale colors a little better. The other thing to remember when you are adding food coloring is that the shade will deepen as the frosting sets.

1. Add the food coloring using a toothpick (Fig. a).

2. Mix into the frosting, ensuring that it is blended evenly (Fig. b).

Filling the cake

Have you ever sliced a cake, filled it with buttercream frosting, put it back together again, and found that none of the layers now seem to fit properly? Here's a little trick to stop that from happening.

1. Before you slice the cake into layers, make a frosting mark down the side of the cake (Fig. c). You can mark it with a knife cut, but I prefer to use frosting since I tend to lose the cut mark in a flurry of crumbs.

2. Slice your cake into layers and spread frosting over the top of the base layer. Place the next layer on top of the bottom one—and here's the trick—line up the frosting marks with each other. If you have a third layer, repeat the procedure, again lining up the frosting marks (Fig. d).

3. Ensure that the layers are even (Fig. e).

Covering with buttercream

When covering a cake with buttercream frosting, cover the sides first. This allows you to hold the top of the cake steady with your other hand without getting too sticky. Spread the frosting around the sides and over the top (Fig. f).

"Setting up" and avoiding crumbs

If you coat your cake with a thin covering of frosting then place it in the refrigerator for a couple of hours to "set up" before covering it with a second, final coating, you will help yourself in two ways. First, it prevents crumbs from being dragged around the surface of the cake. Second, it stops the cake from moving as you frost it. This is especially useful when coating tall cakes such as the Puppet on a String (see pages 56–7) and Candy House (see pages 58–9).

Creating special effects

There are many different effects you can achieve with buttercream frosting by using different techniques, tools, and colors.

Combing

An icing comb is a plastic tool with a serrated edge. As it is run around the outside of a cake, a combed effect is left behind (see Summer Flowers on pages 60–1). If it is wiggled as it is moved around the cake, it will produce a zigzag pattern (see Who's Looking at You? on pages 70–1).

If you want to experiment with combing but don't have a comb, you can very easily make your own. Cut a rectangle out of an ice cream container lid. Cut a few triangles out of one side and you have a homemade icing comb.

Marbling

By partially mixing a little food coloring into the buttercream frosting you get a marbled effect—great for making water effects on novelty cakes.

Multicolored swirls and piping

Achieve a dramatic effect by swirling different colors of frosting onto a cake's surface (see image below left).

You can also pipe with two or three different colors in the piping bag at the same time (Figs. a and b).

A

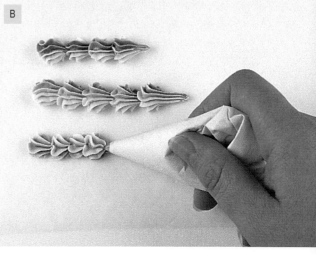

B

Piping

It is very easy to pipe with buttercream frosting, provided the frosting is soft enough to flow easily through the piping nozzle but still holds its shape when piped. If it is too stiff, beat in a little more water.

Because piping with buttercream frosting and royal icing is similar, piping and lettering techniques are described fully in the royal icing section on pages 106–19.

Freezing buttercream

Buttercream frosting freezes extremely well. This quality is exploited in the frozen frosting transfer cakes on pages 62–3 (Baby Face) and 66–7 (Spring Blossom).

If you are covering a cake and find that you have a lot of frosting left over, place it in a plastic bag or plastic container and freeze until needed. When you get ready to use it, let it defrost at room temperature for a few hours. As with all foods, never refreeze buttercream frosting once it has been defrosted.

Another useful fact is that because both sponge cake and buttercream frosting freeze well, you can actually freeze an already frosted cake. Protect it with freezer wrap. Defrosting will take anywhere from 5 to 12 hours depending on the room's temperature. Condensation will form as it defrosts but avoid the temptation to dab it—the cake will dry naturally. Occasionally, strong colors such as black may run a little.

HOW EASY?

All of the cakes in this book can be made successfully by a beginner, but, obviously, there are some cakes that are simpler than others. You will notice that each cake has been allocated a number. This is a quick reference guide to give you a rough idea of how involved the design is and therefore how much time it is likely to take you.

1 Easy

2 Fairly easy

3 Has intricate elements

Templates

All of the templates on pages 41–3 are shown at 90 percent.

Baby Face (see pages 62–3)

Spring Blossom
(see pages 66–7)

Pretty Butterflies
(see pages 50–1)

Buttercream Beauty
(see pages 68–9)

Figure

Border

Celebration Cake

The rolled wafer cookies used here add a pretty pattern to the cake as well as being extremely easy to do. You could substitute chocolate finger cookies if you prefer.

INGREDIENTS
- 8 in. (20cm) round sponge cake (see page 13)
- 2 quantities buttercream frosting (see page 37)
- Small, round, sugarcoated chocolate candies, such as M&M's
- Green paste food coloring
- About 54 rolled wafer cookies (or chocolate finger cookies)

EQUIPMENT
- Carving knife
- Palette knife
- Cake board
- Piping bag (see page 113, but read the tip below first)
- Scissors
- No. 3 piping nozzle
- 1 yd. (1m) lilac ribbon

TECHNIQUES
- Covering with buttercream (see page 38)
- Coloring buttercream (see page 37)
- Making a piping bag (see page 114)
- Piping (see pages 112–9)

1. Split the cake horizontally two or three times and reassemble it, sandwiching the layers together with buttercream frosting.

2. Place the cake on the cake board and spread a thick covering of frosting around the outside of the cake.

3. Place yellow candies—which will form the centers of the flowers—in position on the cake. Make sure there is enough space between them to fit in all the petals.

4. Place six pink or purple candies around each yellow center to form the flowers (Fig. a).

5. To make the leaves, snip a triangle off the end of a piping bag. Insert a No. 3 piping nozzle and then place 1 Tbsp. of green frosting into the bag. Fold the bag to close.

6. Pipe a leaf between each flower. Simply squeeze some frosting out of the end of the bag between two petals. Then release the pressure on the bag and pull away. The frosting should fall away forming a tail (Fig. b).

7. Fill the spaces between the flowers with a few additional candies.

8. Press the rolled wafer cookies or chocolate fingers around the outside of the cake and finish with a ribbon trim. Use a dab of frosting to secure the ribbon at the back of the cake.

Tip If you don't have time to do piping or if you really don't like doing it, use small pieces of green gumdrops instead to make the leaves.

Silver Wedding Cake

Sometimes you're in a hurry or perhaps you've been asked to make an important cake but you've never even wielded a rolling pin before let alone a piping bag. Well, you're in luck! Many specialty stores or online suppliers stock a variety of ready-made decorations. These silver paper rose leaves link beautifully with a silver wedding theme and look lovely and sparkly, too. Even better, there's not a piping bag in sight!

INGREDIENTS
- 7 in. (18cm) square sponge cake (see page 13)
- 1 quantity buttercream frosting (see page 37)
- Edible silver balls

EQUIPMENT
- Carving knife
- Palette knife
- 9 in. (23cm) square cake board
- 5–6 in. (13–15cm) diameter bowl
- Tweezers (optional; see tip below)
- About 64 silver paper rose leaves
- 1 yd. (1m) silver ribbon
- Scissors

TECHNIQUES
- Covering with buttercream (see page 38)

1. Turn the cake upside down. If it won't sit flat on your work surface, turn it back over and slice the top to make it level, then turn it over again.

2. Slice the cake horizontally into two or three layers. Reassemble it, sandwiching the layers together with buttercream frosting.

3. Place the cake on the cake board and spread frosting around the outside of the cake.

4. Carefully place a bowl upside down on top of the frosted cake and just as carefully, lift it off. It should have left a circular impression in the frosting (Fig. a).

5. Using the impression as a guide, stick a circle of silver balls around the top of the cake (Fig. b).

6. Stick the silver rose leaves around the top edge and base of the cake. Make a ribbon bow and place it in the center. Finally, press a few additional balls into the frosting around the cake.

Tip You may find it easier to use a pair of tweezers to handle the silver balls—they can be a little difficult to work with.

Teddy Bear

This cute teddy is very easy to do. If you don't want to use marzipan for the eyes and ears, you could use candy and chocolate buttons for the eyes and nose and small round cookies for the cheeks and ears.

INGREDIENTS
- 8 in. (20cm) square sponge cake (see page 13)
- 1 quantity chocolate buttercream frosting (see page 37)
- 3½ oz. (100g) marzipan
- 1 Tbsp. cocoa powder (or brown paste food coloring)

EQUIPMENT
- Carving knife
- Palette knife
- 12 in. (30cm) round cake board
- Fork
- 1 yd. (1m) red ribbon
- Scissors

TECHNIQUES
- Covering with buttercream (see page 38)
- Creating special effects (see page 39)
- Coloring marzipan (see page 104)

Tips · · · · · · · · · ·

If you are unsure about cutting directly into the cake to make the teddy bear shape, make a template first out of waxed paper. Place the template on top of the cake and cut around it.

Stand birthday cake candles in balls of marzipan or in regular-sized marshmallows (see page 34). With a dab of water, stick these around the cake board away from the cake (particularly away from the ribbon bow).

1. Slice about 2 in. (5cm) off one side of the square cake to make it rectangular. Place the piece you have cut off against the top of the cake to form a "T" shape.

2. Cut out the teddy bear shape (see tips below). The head should be rounded, coming into a point at the neck (Fig. a).

3. Slice the cake and fill with buttercream frosting. Place on the cake board. Spread a thick coating of frosting around the outside of the cake. Using a fork, rough it up to look like fur (Fig. b).

4. Color about 1½ oz. (45g) of marzipan brown by kneading in the cocoa powder or food coloring.

5. Make three ⅛ oz. (5g) dark brown balls for the eyes and nose. Add tiny balls of uncolored marzipan for the highlights. If the highlights won't stick, use a dab of water to hold them in place.

6. Roll out and squash two ½ oz. (15g) balls of uncolored marzipan to make two flattened circles for the cheeks. Place them in position.

7. Add the eyes and the nose. Decorate both cheeks with three tiny flattened brown marzipan dots and add a curved marzipan string for a mouth.

8. To make the ears, roll 1 oz. (30g) of brown marzipan and ½ oz. (15g) of uncolored marzipan into balls. Place the smaller one on top of the larger one and flatten them both together. Cut the flat disk in half and stick one ear on either side of the head.

9. Finish the teddy bear off with a snazzy red bow.

A

B

Pretty Butterflies

An elegant yet simple design that would be suitable for Valentine's Day, an anniversary, or a birthday. If you don't want to make it heart-shaped, the butterflies work just as well on square and round cakes.

INGREDIENTS
- 5–6 sheets edible decorating paper
- Edible dusting powders in assorted colors
- 2 Tbsp. confectioners' sugar
- 7 in. (18cm) square sponge cake (see page 13)
- 2 quantities pink buttercream frosting (see page 37)

EQUIPMENT
- Scissors
- Pencil
- Saucer
- Waxed or tracing paper
- Carving knife
- Palette knife
- 10 in. (25cm) round cake board

TECHNIQUES
- Coloring buttercream (see page 37)
- Covering with buttercream (see page 38)

1. To make the butterflies, you can cut them out freehand or use the templates supplied on page 42. If cutting freehand, simply fold a piece of edible decorating paper in half and cut out half a butterfly shape. If using the templates, make sure the edge of the template lines up with the decorating paper fold. Cut inside the pencil lines (Fig. a). Open out the butterfly and place to one side. Make about 40.

2. To color the butterflies, place some dusting powders on the edge of a saucer and some confectioners' sugar in the center. Using your finger, mix a little dusting powder with a little confectioners' sugar, and spread onto a butterfly's wings using a light circular motion. If the decorating paper is rough side up, a textured effect will appear. Color the paper on one side only. Decorate all of the butterflies and place to one side.

3. Trace around the heart-shaped cake template on page 83 and cut out. Place the template on top of the cake and cut out the shape (Fig. b).

4. Slice the cake into two or three layers and sandwich the layers together with buttercream frosting. Place the cake on the cake board and spread a thick covering of frosting around the top and sides.

5. Gently press the butterflies into the frosting all over the cake.

Tips

You can prepare your butterflies weeks ahead if you wish.

Be very careful if using candles on a cake like this since the decorating paper could easily catch fire. If you really want to use candles, stick butterflies around the sides of the cake only and place the candles on top.

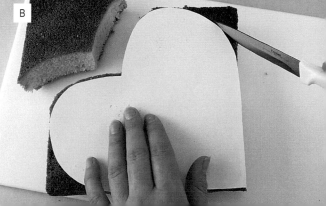

Take the Train

Incredible though it may seem, there is absolutely no baking involved in this cake. You can buy all of the ingredients at the supermarket (although you can also use your own homemade cakes if you wish). The only thing you need to make is some buttercream frosting for sticking the elements together.

INGREDIENTS
- 6 mini-chocolate Swiss rolls
- 1 quantity buttercream frosting (see page 37)
- 1 large chocolate Swiss roll
- 1 Battenburg cake (or similar—any rectangular chunk of cake will do!)
- 7 plain, round cookies
- 2 white chocolate buttons
- Assorted small, round, colored candies, such as M&M's
- 1 red jellybean
- About 14 chocolate finger cookies
- 1 mini-jam Swiss roll
- 2 breadsticks
- ½ cup (30g/1 oz.) shredded unsweetened coconut
- Black and green paste food coloring

EQUIPMENT
- 10 in. (25cm) square cake board
- Carving knife
- Palette knife
- Fork

TECHNIQUES
- Coloring buttercream (see page 37)
- Creating special effects (see page 39)

1. Place six mini-Swiss rolls in a diagonal line on the cake board. Fix in place with dabs of buttercream frosting.

2. Place the large Swiss roll on top so that it overhangs the rolls at the front. Leave enough room at the other end to stand the Battenburg cake up, so trim the Swiss roll to size if necessary. The roll represents the engine.

3. Stand the Battenburg cake upright on the mini-rolls, behind the engine and fix in place with frosting (Fig. a). The Battenburg cake is the driver's cab.

4. Stick three plain cookies along both sides of the engine to form the wheels. Stick another one on the front of the train ready for the face.

5. To make the face, use two white chocolate buttons and two small round brown candies for the eyes. Use a pink candy for the nose and a red jellybean for the mouth. Stick in place with frosting (Fig. b).

6. Stick about six chocolate fingers on top of the driver's cab and candies around the edges of the engine and cab.

7. Stick a mini-jam roll funnel upright on top of the engine and a breadstick horizontally along each set of wheels, using frosting as a glue.

8. Use about four chocolate fingers to make short sections of track in front of and behind the train. Fix in place with frosting (Fig. c).

9. Place the coconut into a bowl and mix some black food coloring into it using a spoon or your fingers. Carefully sprinkle the colored coconut "gravel" between the tracks. (You can leave this step out if you find it too time-consuming.)

10. Color the leftover frosting green and smear it around the rest of the cake board. Use a fork to rough it up a little to resemble grass.

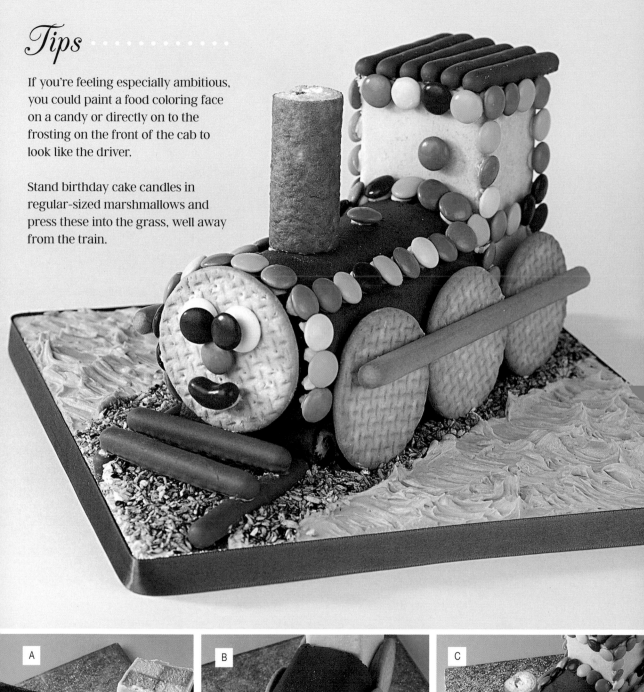

Tips

If you're feeling especially ambitious, you could paint a food coloring face on a candy or directly on to the frosting on the front of the cab to look like the driver.

Stand birthday cake candles in regular-sized marshmallows and press these into the grass, well away from the train.

A

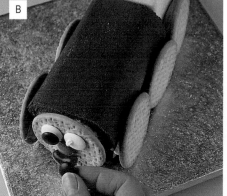

B

C

Buttercream Flowers

This star piping technique is easy to master and produces an interesting texture as well as an attractive design. This cake would be suitable for all sorts of occasions—birthdays, Mother's day, Easter—to name but a few.

INGREDIENTS
- 7 in. (18cm) round sponge cake (see page 13)
- 2 quantities buttercream frosting (see page 37)
- 1 strand uncooked spaghetti
- Pink, yellow, and green paste food coloring

EQUIPMENT
- Carving knife
- Palette knife
- 9 in. (23cm) round cake board
- Star piping nozzles
- Piping bags (see page 113)
- Small bowls for mixing food coloring

TECHNIQUES
- Filling the cake (see page 38)
- Coloring buttercream (see page 37)
- Making a piping bag (see page 114)
- Piping stars (see page 116)

Tip

This cake can be decorated and then frozen. Store it carefully in the freezer to avoid damage and defrost gently at room temperature for 6 to 8 hours.

1. Level the top of the cake and turn it upside-down. Split the cake horizontally and fill the layers with buttercream frosting.

2. Place the cake onto the cake board and spread a thin coating of frosting over the outside of the cake.

3. Using a strand of spaghetti, gently score the outline of the pattern you are going to pipe into the frosting. If you go wrong, smooth the frosting over and start again. Draw wiggly lines for the stems and a circle surrounded by petals for the flowers (Fig. a). These lines will be hidden by the piping.

4. Place a star nozzle into a piping bag. Put about a 1 Tbsp. of pink frosting into the bag and fold the end of the bag to close it.

5. Pipe a star on the edge of one of the flower centers. Just squeeze a bit of frosting out of the end of the nozzle, release the pressure, and pull the bag upward, away from the cake. Pipe a ring of stars around the outside of one of the flower centers then fill in the middle. Repeat on the other two flower centers (Fig. b).

6. Repeat the procedure on the flower petals using yellow frosting. Then pipe and fill in the stems and the leaves with green. Finally, fill in the outside of the cake using uncolored frosting.

7. To decorate the cake board, pipe a line of green stars around the base of the cake. Follow this with a ring of uncolored frosting, then a line of pink.

8. To finish, pipe a few single pink stars over the cake.

Puppet on a String

Now admit it, you never knew a breadstick could be this useful, did you? Here, breadsticks make great handles for dangling a puppet on a string.

INGREDIENTS

- 8 in. (20cm) square sponge cake (see page 13)
- 1 quantity buttercream frosting (see page 37)
- 2 breadsticks
- 4 lollipops
- Red string licorice
- 1 ice cream cone
- 1 round cookie
- 2 strands of fruit leather candy for hair
- White and milk chocolate buttons (or small melting wafers)
- Assorted candies, such as jellybeans and gumdrops, for decorating cake and cake board

EQUIPMENT

- Carving knife
- 8 in. (20cm) square cake board
- Palette knife
- Scissors
- Small sharp knife

TECHNIQUES

- Covering with buttercream (see page 38)
- "Setting up" and avoiding crumbs (see page 38)

1. Slice about 2 in. (5cm) off one side of the square cake to form an 8 x 6 in. (20 x 1cm) rectangle.

2. Stand the cake upright on one of the shorter sides. Use what was originally the flat base of the cake to form a smooth front.

3. If you want to fill the cake with buttercream frosting, slice the cake horizontally into two or three layers and reassemble it using frosting.

4. Stand the cake diagonally on the cake board and spread frosting over the sides and top.

5. If you have time, place the cake in the refrigerator for about an hour so that the frosting can harden. Spread another coating of frosting over the outside of the cake when you remove it from the refrigerator so that the candies have something to stick to.

6. Lay two crossed breadsticks on top of the cake. Use dabs of frosting to hold them in place.

7. Press two lollipops into the lower part of the cake for the legs.

8. Cut two pieces of licorice, about 10 in. (25cm) long, for the strings. Press them into the cake so they run from a lollipop foot, up the cake, and over the top of the breadsticks. Trim if necessary and press the ends into the frosting on top of the cake (Fig. a).

9. Carefully cut the pointed end off an ice cream cone and slice the cone in half. Place it over the top of the legs to form a dress. Add a cookie for the head (Fig. b).

10. Add two more lollipops for arms and licorice strings leading from the arms and head to the breadsticks.

11. Use a couple of fruit leather strands to make the hair, pressing them gently into the frosting so that they stay in place.

12. Use two white and two milk chocolate buttons for the eyes. Stick them onto the cookie face with dabs of frosting. Add a tiny frosting dot for a highlight (Fig. c).

13. For the mouth cut a milk chocolate button in half and stick in place. Cut four white chocolate buttons in half. Use two to make the collar and five to make a frill around the bottom of the dress. Stick two milk chocolate buttons on the front of the dress. Make a licorice bow and stick it on top of the head.

14. Smear the cake board with frosting and press candies all around the outside edges of the cake and over the cake board.

Tips ·········

To make a boy puppet, use a second round cookie to make a body instead of the dress. Decorate with a couple of chocolate buttons. Give him shorter hair and leave the bow off.

Either stand birthday cake candles on the top of the cake or stand in marshmallows and stick them onto the cake board with buttercream frosting.

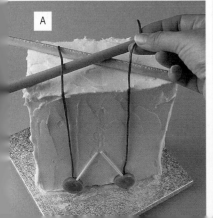

A

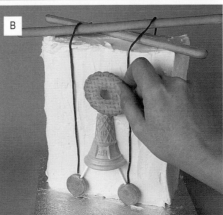

B

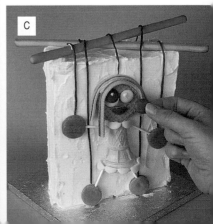

C

Candy House

Just watch your child's face light up with delight when this fairy-tale house arrives on the table. It may look terribly complicated at first glance but in fact it is very easy to assemble. If you are planning to incorporate candles into the design, please read the tip right before you start.

INGREDIENTS

- 10 in. (25cm) square sponge cake (see page 13)
- 1 quantity buttercream frosting (see page 37; color 4 Tbsp. green for the grass, flavor the rest with chocolate)
- Green paste food coloring
- Milk and white chocolate finger cookies
- 3 thin slices Battenburg cake or square cookies
- Lady fingers
- At least 15 wafers
- Assorted small candies and mini-marshmallows for brickwork
- 1 mini-Swiss roll
- Raindrop candies or sprinkles for gravel
- Coconut mushrooms (available online)

EQUIPMENT

- Carving knife
- Palette knife
- 12 in. (30cm) round cake board
- Fork

1. If your cake has a very rounded top, slice a bit off to level it, then cut the entire cake in half diagonally.

2. Place the two triangular halves on top of each other. Slice a small triangle off each end (Fig. a).

3. Sandwich the layers together with buttercream frosting. Stand the cake upright on the cake board and spread a thin coating of frosting over the outside of the cake (Fig. b). If you have time, place the cake in the refrigerator for an hour.

4. Spread a second, thicker layer of frosting over the outside of the cake. This will act as glue for the decorations.

5. Place four chocolate fingers upright in the center to make a door. Press three thin slices of Battenburg cake or square cookies in position for the windows. Add a couple of lady fingers for steps and window ledges.

6. Then starting from the bottom, stick a line of overlapping wafers or graham cracker halves up both sides of the roof (Fig. c). Press one wafer or graham cracker over the door to make a porch.

7. Fill in the brickwork by pressing candies or mini-marshmallows into the frosting around the house. If you want to save a bit of time and use fewer candies, leave the back of the house plain, covered with frosting only.

8. To make the chimney, slice a small diagonal section off a mini-Swiss roll. Stick it on the roof with a blob of frosting and add a small candy for the chimney pot.

9. Stick a line of candies along the ridge of the roof and a candy for a doorknob. Decorate the roof with a few additional candies if you wish. Again, use frosting as glue.

10. Smear the green frosting around the cake board. Use a fork to rough up the frosting to make it look like grass.

11. To make the fencing, cut about 15 lady fingers in half and stand them upright in the grass all around the house.

12. Sprinkle raindrop candies or rainbow sprinkles in front of the door to make a path.

13. Place a few extra candies or coconut mushrooms on both sides of the door.

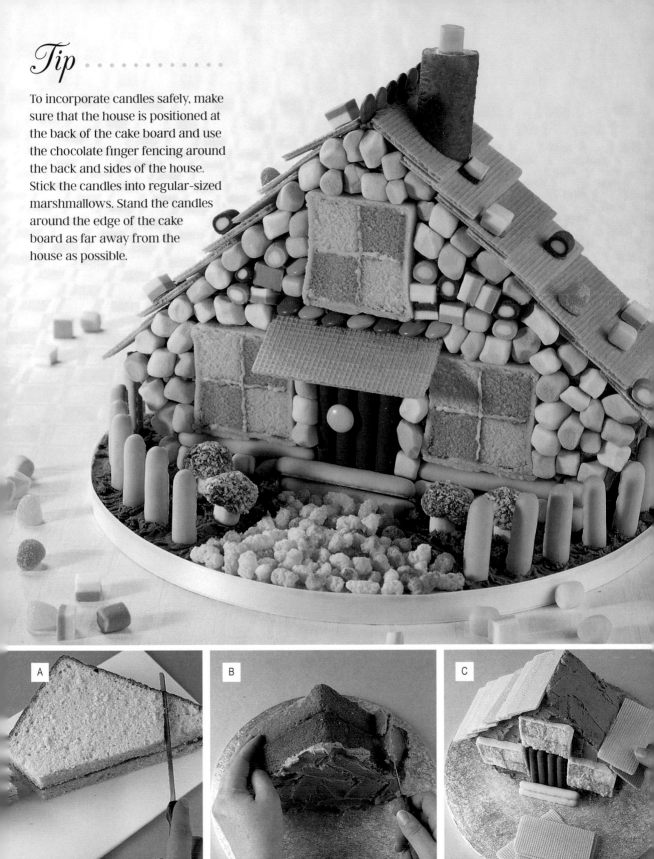

Tip · · · · · · · · ·

To incorporate candles safely, make sure that the house is positioned at the back of the cake board and use the chocolate finger fencing around the back and sides of the house. Stick the candles into regular-sized marshmallows. Stand the candles around the edge of the cake board as far away from the house as possible.

A

B

C

Summer Flowers

All the piping on this cake was done using a No. 4 piping nozzle, which has got a large round hole in the end. If you don't have one, you can achieve a similar effect by making a piping bag, filling it, and snipping a tiny triangle off the end.

INGREDIENTS
- 2 quantities buttercream frosting (see page 37)
- 6 in. (15cm) round sponge cake (see page 13)
- Yellow, pink, and green paste food coloring

EQUIPMENT
- Piping bags (see page 113)
- No. 4 piping nozzle
- Waxed paper
- Carving knife
- Palette knife
- 8 in. (20cm) round cake board
- Small bowls for mixing colors
- Serrated icing comb (optional)

TECHNIQUES
- Making a piping bag (see page 114)
- Filling the cake (see page 38)
- Covering with buttercream (see page 38)
- Coloring buttercream (see page 37)
- "Setting up" and avoiding crumbs (see page 38)
- Combing (see page 39)

1. Place about 2 Tbsp. of buttercream frosting in a piping bag fitted with a No. 4 piping nozzle. Pipe five large dots on a sheet of waxed paper in a flower formation (Fig. a). Make about 30 and chill them in the refrigerator for a few hours.

2. In the meantime prepare the cake. Split the cake into two or three layers and reassemble it, filling the layers with frosting. Color all but 5 Tbsp. of the frosting yellow.

3. Place the cake on the cake board and spread a thin coating of yellow frosting all over the outside of the cake. Put in the refrigerator for an hour or so to "set up." This will stop crumbs from getting caught up in the frosting and spoiling the finish of the cake later.

4. When ready, spread a thicker coating of yellow frosting over the sides. Run a serrated icing comb around the sides of the cake (optional).

5. Spread additional yellow frosting over the top of the cake and run the icing comb over it (optional; Fig. b).

6. Using a palette knife, spread a thin coating of yellow frosting over the cake board (Fig. c).

7. When the flowers are set, carefully lift them off the waxed paper with a knife and stick them around the top edge of the cake with a blob of frosting. Stick a cluster of three flowers in the center and the rest around the base of the cake.

8. Color about 1 Tbsp. of frosting pink and place in a piping bag with a No. 4 piping nozzle. Fold the bag to close. Pipe five dots in the center of each flower. Wash the nozzle.

9. Color the rest of the frosting green and place in another piping bag with a No. 4 piping nozzle. To pipe the leaves between the flowers, simply squeeze the bag, release the pressure, and pull away. The frosting will fall away, leaving a tapering tail behind.

Variation

The version below still conveys a feeling of freshness even though it has a lot fewer flowers on it. There is no combing involved and just three flowers in the center. Leaves were piped around the top and base of the cake. Pink dots, in groups of three, were then piped both among the leaves and around the top and sides of the cake.

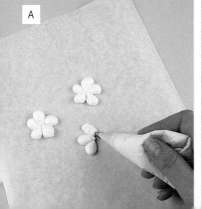

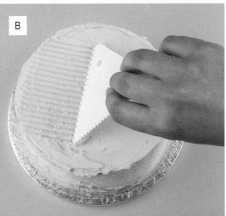

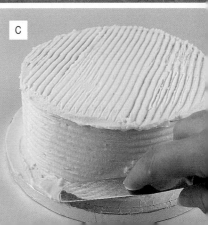

Baby Face

A technique called frozen buttercream transfer is a simple way to put pictures on the tops of cakes. Note that you will need to have a freezer in order to make the transfer. This cake would make a cute christening cake or a first birthday cake.

INGREDIENTS
- 2 quantities buttercream frosting (see page 37)
- Black, pink, yellow, and blue paste food coloring
- 6 in. (15cm) square sponge cake (see page 13)
- 1 lb. mini-jelly gumdrops

EQUIPMENT
- Pencil
- Waxed or tracing paper
- Scissors
- 2 thin cake boards or pieces of card (bigger than the design)
- Plastic wrap
- Masking tape
- Piping bags (see page 113)
- No. 2 piping nozzle
- Small bowls for mixing food coloring
- Dressmaker's pin
- Carving knife
- Palette knife

TECHNIQUES
- Making a piping bag (see page 114)
- Coloring buttercream (see page 37)
- Piping (see pages 112–9)
- Filling the cake (see page 38)
- Covering with buttercream (see page 38)

1. Trace the baby design on page 41 onto waxed or tracing paper. If you want to make a cake of a different size, use a photocopier to alter the size of the design.

2. Place the design on a thin cake board and put a sheet of plastic wrap over the top. Use a tiny bit of tape at the edges to hold it in place if you wish.

3. Place about 1 Tbsp. of black buttercream frosting into a piping bag fitted with a No. 2 piping nozzle. Trace the picture and fill in the baby's mouth.

4. Place some pink frosting in a piping bag. Close the end and snip a tiny triangle off the pointed end. Fill in the outline of the picture. Refer to the photograph opposite to help you put the colors in the right places.

5. Repeat the procedure with the blue and yellow frosting and fill in the background of the picture with uncolored frosting.

6. When you have finished the picture, carefully remove the tape from the corners and gently lay a second sheet of plastic wrap over the top of the design.

7. Place a second thin cake board on top of the pile and carefully turn the entire thing over. Gently press down and squash the boards together.

8. Remove what are now the top cake board and the traced design. Using your finger, gently rub over the plastic wrap in a circular motion to get rid of the piping marks (Fig. a). Prick any air bubbles with a pin.

9. When you have finished, place the second cake board back on top of the picture and place in the freezer for at least an hour.

10. Cut the cake in half horizontally and sandwich the layers together with frosting. Place the cake onto the cake board and spread a smooth covering of frosting over the top and sides of the cake.

11. When frozen, remove the cake board and plastic wrap from the back of the design.

12. Carefully lift the design by the edges of the plastic wrap and lay the frosted side on top of the cake. Peel off the plastic wrap (Fig. b).

13. Spread frosting over the cake board and press a line of jelly gumdrops around the edges of the cake. Place a few candies in the corners and at the sides of the cake, and scatter some on the cake board.

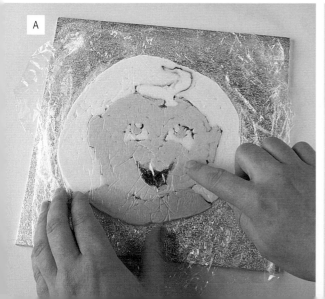

A

B

Bouquet of Hyacinths

This cake is a perfect demonstration of how limiting the number of colors on a cake can actually enhance the design. If in doubt, keep it simple. Practice piping the stars a few times first before you attempt the real thing.

INGREDIENTS
- 6 in. (15cm) round sponge cake (see page 13)
- 2 quantities buttercream frosting (see page 37)
- Green, purple, and blue paste food coloring

EQUIPMENT
- Carving knife
- Palette knife
- 8 in. (20cm) round cake board
- No. 4 piping nozzle
- Scissors
- Piping bags (see page 113)
- Small bowls for mixing colors
- Star piping nozzle

TECHNIQUES
- Filling the cake (see page 38)
- Covering with buttercream (see page 38)
- Coloring buttercream (see page 37)
- Making a piping bag (see page 114)
- Piping stars (see page 116)

1. Level the top of the cake and split it horizontally into two or three layers. Reassemble the cake, filling the layers with buttercream frosting.

2. Place the cake on the cake board and spread frosting around the top and sides.

3. Place a No. 4 piping nozzle in a piping bag. Color about 2 Tbsp. of frosting green and place in the bag. Fold over the end of the bag to close it and pipe lines for the stems and leaves around the sides of the cake (Fig. a). Pipe a cluster of stems and leaves on top of the cake.

4. Color about 2 Tbsp. of purple frosting and place in a bag fitted with the star piping nozzle. Pipe a line of stars either side of one of the stems on top of the cake (Fig. b). Repeat on alternate flower stems all around the sides of the cake.

5. When you have piped all of the purple flowers, pipe a line of stars around the top edge of the cake.

6. Wash and dry the star piping nozzle and place into a second piping bag. Color about 2 Tbsp. of the frosting blue and place into the bag. Pipe the remaining flowers and ring on top of the cake (Fig. c).

Variation

You can use the same star piping technique to make simple daisy flowers, too. Pipe a central yellow star, then pipe five or six pink ones around the outside.

Spring Blossom

This cake is made using the same frozen transfer method as Baby Face (see pages 62–3), but piping and combing techniques are also used (see tip on following page).

INGREDIENTS
- 2 quantities buttercream frosting (see page 37)
- Black, yellow, pink, green, and brown paste food coloring
- 7 in. (18cm) round sponge cake (see page 13)

EQUIPMENT
- Pencil
- Waxed or tracing paper
- Scissors
- 2 thin cake boards or pieces of card board (bigger than the design)
- Plastic wrap
- Masking tape
- Piping bags (see page 113)
- No. 2 piping nozzle
- Small bowls for mixing food coloring
- Dressmaker's pin
- Carving knife
- Palette knife
- Serrated icing comb (optional)
- Star piping nozzle

TECHNIQUES
- Coloring buttercream (see page 37)
- Making a piping bag (see page 114)
- Piping (see page 112–9)
- Filling the cake (see page 38)
- Covering with buttercream (see page 38)
- Combing (see page 39)

1. Trace the flower design on page 42 on to waxed or tracing paper. If you want to make a cake of a different size, alter the size of the design using a photocopier.

2. Place the design onto a thin cake board and place a sheet of plastic wrap over the top. Use a tiny bit of tape at the edges to hold it in place.

3. Place about 1 Tbsp. of black buttercream frosting into a piping bag fitted with a No. 2 piping nozzle. Pipe over the outline of the picture (Fig. a).

4. Place some yellow frosting in a piping bag. Close and snip a tiny triangle off the end. Fill in the design using the appropriate colors (Fig. b). Use uncolored frosting for the background.

5. Carefully remove the tape from the corners and gently lay a second sheet of plastic wrap over the top of the design. Place a second thin cake board on top of the pile and carefully turn the entire thing over. Gently press down and squash the boards together.

6. Remove what are now the top cake board and the traced design. Using your finger, gently rub the plastic wrap in a circular motion to get rid of the piping marks. Use a pin to prick any air bubbles that might develop.

7. Place the second cake board back on top and put in the freezer for at least an hour.

8. Cut the cake in half horizontally and sandwich the layers together with frosting. Place the cake on the cake board and spread quite a thick coating of frosting over the sides of the cake. If you wish, run an icing comb around the outside of the cake to make a pattern (see Fig. b on page 61). Spread a thin coating of frosting over the top of the cake.

9. When the design has frozen, take it out of the freezer and remove the top cake board and sheet of plastic wrap from the back of the design.

10. Carefully lift the design by the edges of the film and lay the frosted side on top of the cake. Peel off the plastic wrap.

11. Pipe a line of shells around the top and bottom edges of the cake and pipe a few pink stars on the side if you wish.

Tip To simplify this design, stick gumdrops or other small candies around the edges of the cake instead of piping and combing.

Buttercream Beauty

This cake may look intricate, but it's actually very easy to put together. The design is simply cut out of edible decorating paper and slotted into the buttercream frosting. The decorations can be made weeks in advance if you want to plan ahead.

INGREDIENTS
- 5–6 sheets of edible decorating paper
- Edible blue and pink dusting powder
- 2 Tbsp. confectioners' sugar
- 8 in. (20cm) round sponge cake (see page 13)
- 2 quantities buttercream frosting (see page 37)

EQUIPMENT
- Pencil
- Scissors
- Saucer
- Paintbrush
- Carving knife
- Palette knife
- 10 in. (25cm) round cake board
- Tweezers

1. With the smooth side of the edible decorating paper uppermost, lightly trace over the figure templates on page 43 with a pencil. Cut out just inside the pencil lines.

2. Fold a piece of decorating paper in half and line the folded edge up to the edge of the border template. Trace and cut out a border. Open it out and cut out inside the pencil lines. Keep the heart shape from the middle. Make 16.

3. Tip a little blue and pink dusting powder onto a saucer. Place a little confectioners' sugar in the center. Using your finger, rub some dust into some confectioners' sugar and then onto the decorating paper (smooth side up). Using a light circular motion (Fig. a), just color along the edge of each piece of the decorating paper. When coloring the border sections, color eight pink and the rest blue. Also color all the cut-out hearts and the shapes for the figure.

4. Color two decorating paper rectangles about 4 x 2 in. (10 x 5cm), one blue and the other pink. Cut these into thin strips. Wind the strips around a paintbrush handle to curl them (Fig. b). When finished, place all the decorating paper sections to one side and prepare the cake.

5. Level the top of the cake and turn it upside-down so the base becomes the top. Slice it two or three times horizontally and fill the layers with frosting.

6. Place the cake onto the cake board and spread frosting around the top and sides.

7. Insert the paper decorations as soon as you've finished coating the cake so that they stick securely. Using the tweezers, place the main dress section in position and poke the neck section into the frosting to hold it in place. Insert the two petticoat sections and foot beneath it. Then add the two arms and the bonnet pieces.

8. Place two blue and two pink edging sections alternatively around the edge of the cake. Position another ring of four in front of them. Repeat around the base of the cake. Place the cut-out hearts around the border so that they hide the joins.

9. Stick some of the decorative paper twirls on top of the cake and the rest into the sides.

Tips ·······

To save time you could use just four border sections around both the top and base.

Be careful with candles on this design because the edible decorating paper could catch fire. If you do use candles, place them securely on top of the cake, away from any paper twirls and blow them out as soon as possible.

A

B

Who's Looking at You?

The combed effect used on the sides and lid of the box make it look as though it's made of wicker. If you find the prospect of combing a bit daunting, cover the box with smooth buttercream frosting and decorate with a few candies instead.

INGREDIENTS

- 6 in. (15cm) square sponge cake (see page 13)
- 2 quantities buttercream frosting (see page 37)
- Blue and black paste food coloring
- 1 oz. (30g) white fondant or two white marshmallows (see tips below)
- ½ oz. (15g) black fondant or two chocolate buttons

EQUIPMENT

- Carving knife
- Palette knife
- 8 in. (20cm) square cake board
- Serrated icing comb (optional)
- Piping bag (see page 113)
- Star piping nozzle (optional)
- 6 in. (15cm) thin square cake board
- Scissors
- 1 yd. (1m) ribbon

TECHNIQUES

- Filling the cake (see page 38)
- Covering with buttercream (see page 38)
- Coloring buttercream (see page 37)
- Combing (see page 39)

1. Level the top of the cake and turn it upside down. Slice it horizontally two or three times. Reassemble the cake, filling the layers with buttercream frosting, and place the cake on the cake board.

2. Color about half of the frosting pale blue. Spread a thin covering over the sides of the cake. If possible, place the cake in the refrigerator for about an hour.

3. Remove the cake from the refrigerator and spread a thicker layer of blue frosting over the sides.

4. Holding the serrated edge of the comb vertically, run it along the sides of the cake, wiggling it slightly as you go to make the wavy pattern (Fig. a). Color about 3 Tbsp. of the frosting black. Spread this over the top of the cake.

5. Place about 2 Tbsp. of colorless frosting in a piping bag fitted with the star nozzle. Pipe shells around the edges of the cake.

6. Make two white fondant balls for the eyes. Stick on two black fondant disks and two tiny white balls for highlights with water. Place the eyes on the top of the cake (Fig. b).

7. To make the lid, smear pale blue frosting over the thin cake board and use the serrated comb to make a wiggly pattern.

8. Place the lid in position on the cake and pipe around the edges.

9. To finish off, make a jaunty-looking bow and stick it on the top of the cake with a small blob of frosting.

Tips Another way to make the eyes is to stick a chocolate button onto a white marshmallow and add a dot of frosting as a highlight.

If you want to put candles on this cake, position the cake as far back on the cake board as you can. Stand the candles in either fondant balls or marshmallows on the board at the front. Make sure that the tail of the ribbon is not dangling too close to any of the candles.

FONDANT

Basically, fondant is an edible form of modeling clay. Sometimes called fondant or ready-to-roll icing, it is simple to make and easy to use. It is also available ready-made from supermarkets, specialty stores, or online suppliers (see Suppliers on page 165).

Recipe

There is a slight risk of salmonella from using raw egg (see note on page 5). If you prefer, you can use dried egg whites. Refer to the instructions for mixing on the package.

INGREDIENTS
(Amounts for 1 quantity)
- 1 lb. 2 oz. (500g) confectioners' sugar
- 1 egg white (or equivalent amount of dried egg white, reconstituted)
- 2 Tbsp. (30ml) corn syrup

1. Place the sugar into a bowl. Make a well in the center.

2. Tip the egg white and corn syrup into the well and stir in using a wooden spoon.

3. Finish binding the fondant together using your hands. Knead until all the sugar is incorporated and the fondant feels silky and smooth.

4. Double-wrap in two small plastic bags to prevent it from drying out. The fondant can be used immediately and does not require refrigeration. Use within a week.

Using fondant

Fondant will harden as it is exposed to the air so if you open a package and use just a little, rewrap what's left over in a small plastic bag to prevent it from drying out. Keep unused bags of fondant in a plastic container. It does not need to be kept in the refrigerator.

When you are rolling it out, always roll it on confectioners' sugar, never use flour or cornstarch. Keep a bowl of confectioners' sugar handy to stop your fingers from getting sticky. Don't worry about getting your creation "dusty" with the sugar. Simply brush marks away with a soft, damp paintbrush at the end.

When you are making models, you can use water to stick the pieces together. Never soak the fondant; apply just a dab with a soft paintbrush to make the surface of the fondant tacky. Try to avoid getting drips of water on the fondant because they will dissolve the surface, leaving an unsightly watermark behind.

This cake is a variation on Hearts and Ribbons (see pages 92–3). Cover the cake and press the heart pattern in the fondant. Using about 2 yds. (2m) of ribbon, pass it over the cake, and tie under the cake board. Bring the ends back up and tie into a bow on top of the cake.

QUANTITY GUIDE

The amount of fondant you need to coat a cake can vary, depending on how thick you like your icing to be. Here is a guide to give you a rough idea.

Round cake	6 in. (15cm)	7 in. (18cm)	8 in. (20cm)	9 in. (23cm)	10 in. (25cm)	11 in. (28cm)	12 in. (30cm)	—
Square cake	—	6 in. (15cm)	7 in. (18cm)	8 in. (20cm)	9 in. (23cm)	10 in. (25cm)	11 in. (28cm)	12 in. (30cm)
Amount of fondant	1 lb. 2 oz. (500g)	1 lb. 5 oz. (650g)	1 lb. 10 oz. (800g)	2 lbs. (900g)	2½ lbs. (1.1kg)	3 lbs. (1.4kg)	3½ lbs. (1.6kg)	4 lbs. (1.8kg)

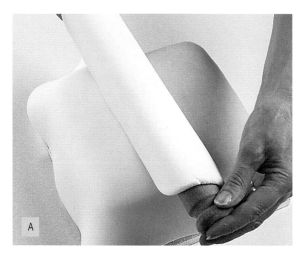

A

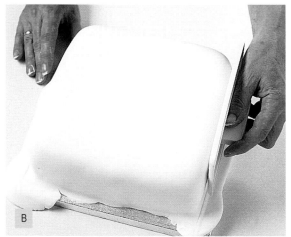

B

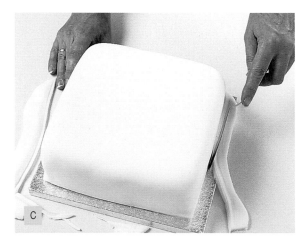

C

Covering a cake with fondant

Before covering a sponge cake with fondant, cover it completely on the outside with either a coating of buttercream frosting (see page 37) or apricot jam. This will hold the fondant in place.

If you are using a fruitcake, it should first be covered with a layer of marzipan (see page 101). When done, brush the surface of the marzipan with clear alcohol, such as vodka, or cooled, boiled water. This will make it tacky so the fondant will adhere to it.

1. Dust your work surface with confectioners' sugar to stop the fondant from sticking. Knead the fondant until it feels soft and pliable.

2. Roll it out to a thickness of about ¼ in. (5mm). Don't roll it too thinly or it will show up any irregularities in the cake's surface.

3. Lift the fondant and place over the top of the cake. You can do this by either sliding your hands—palms flat and facing upward underneath the fondant—or with a rolling pin (Fig. a).

4. To avoid air from getting trapped underneath, start with the top and smooth the fondant into position. A cake smoother is useful here to iron out lumps and bumps (Fig. b). If you do get an air bubble, prick it with a dressmaker's pin.

5. Cut away any excess fondant from around the base (Fig. c).

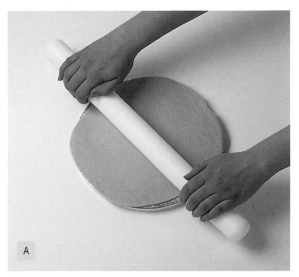

A

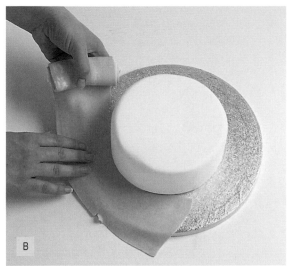

B

Covering cake boards with fondant

Covering the exposed cake board around the base of the cake can often create a neater design. Here are three ways to do this.

The all-in-one method

This is the easiest method of covering a cake board.

1. Lightly moisten the entire cake board with water and begin to roll out a ball of fondant on your work surface.

2. Lift and place the fondant on the cake board and roll it up to and over the edges of the board (Fig. a). Trim the edges so they are neat. The covered cake can now be placed on top.

The bandage method

This method is used after the cake itself has been covered and is in position on the cake board.

1. Moisten the exposed cake board with a little water.

2. Measure the circumference of the cake and cut out a long, thin fondant strip, a bit longer than that measurement and wider than the exposed board.

3. Slide a knife along under the fondant to ensure that it's not stuck to the work surface and then roll up the fondant like a loose bandage.

4. Starting from the back, unwind the bandage around the board (Fig. b). Trim the join and edges so they are neat.

The four-strip method

This is a useful way to cover the cake board around a square or rectangular cake.

1. Moisten the cake board with a little water.

2. Thinly roll out the fondant and cut out four strips, each slightly longer and wider than the exposed sides of the cake board.

3. Lay one strip along each side of the cake. Make a diagonal cut from the edge of the board to the edge of the cake at each corner and peel away any excess fondant (Fig. c).

4. The fondant should now form a neat join at each corner. Trim the edges so they are neat.

The board for this cake, Frosted Flowers (see pages 88-9), was covered using the bandage method.

A

Coloring fondant

You can purchase pre-dyed fondant from specialty stores or online suppliers (see Suppliers on page 165), but it is easy to color your own. It is best to use paste or gel colors rather than liquid ones. The pastes are thicker and won't make the fondant soggy.

1. Apply dabs of paste food coloring with a toothpick (Fig. a).

2. Knead the color in until all of the fondant is an even color (Fig. b).

As well as using food color, you can also knead different colors of fondant together to get different shades; for example you can mix white with black to make gray. For a flat matte color, knead until all the color has been mixed in and no streaks are visible.

B

Creating different effects with color

You can achieve a variety of looks with fondant, from wood grain to marbled. Try using food coloring like watercolor paints to create different shades.

Wood grain effect

Achieving a wood grain effect is simple, and much like marbling (below), it can be done in two ways.

1. Roll some white fondant into a sausage shape and apply some streaks of brown food coloring (Fig. a) or small pieces of brown fondant.

2. Fold the fondant in half and roll it into a sausage again. Keep repeating this folding and rolling process, and you will soon see a wood grain effect appear (Fig. b).

3. Stop before it becomes a solid color and roll out the fondant. If you go too far, add some small pieces of white fondant and repeat the process.

Marbling

You can either apply a few dabs of food coloring and only partially knead it in, or you can use two different colors of fondant. This method is explained below (Fig. c).

1. Take a lump of white fondant and a smaller ball of the appropriate vein color. Break the smaller lump into pieces and press onto the white.

2. Carefully roll and knead the two together until you see a marbled effect occurring. If you go too far and it all turns one color, reverse the process by adding a little more white.

3. If you are using black and white fondant like this, then you can pull off small pieces and roll them into balls. These balls make excellent fondant pebbles or rocks and can even be used as candleholders.

A

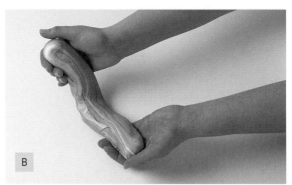

B

C

Multicolored effects

Another easy effect can be achieved by breaking three or four different colors of fondant into lumps, then lightly pressing and rolling them together (Fig. d). This method is useful if you're putting together a groovy disco or party cake!

D

Painting on fondant

If possible, let the cake harden overnight before painting on it. This will make the surface of the cake less prone to dents if you lean on it. You must only use food coloring for painting.

1. Brush the surface of the cake with a pastry brush to get rid of any confectioners' sugar, which might cause the color to bleed.

2. Paint a light outline on the cake first using some watered-down food coloring, then fill it in.

3. Use the food coloring like watercolor paints, mixing them in a palette to get different shades (Fig. e). If you want to paint a black outline around the images, do this after you have painted the middle. If you paint the black outlines first, the black will bleed into the central color.

4. If you make a mistake, gently dab and break up the error with a soft paintbrush dipped into clean water. Wipe away the mistake with a clean, damp cloth.

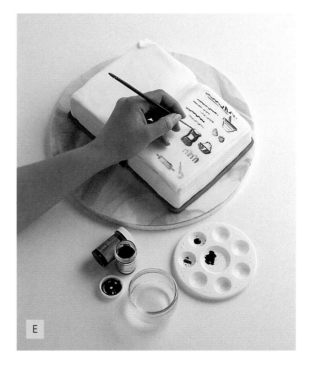

E

A

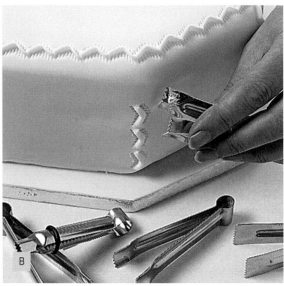

B

Creating easy effects with tools
Crimping
Crimping tools are available from specialty stores or online suppliers (see Suppliers on page 165). Inexpensive and easy to use, they are a simple and quick way to give your fondant cakes neat, decorative edges. (See the "letter A" cake on page 25 and the "number 3" cake on page 29.)

1. Place the crimper on the edge of the cake, then squeeze firmly and release (Fig. a).

2. The crimper pinches the fondant, leaving behind a pattern (Fig. b).

Twisting strands
If you're not interested in piping, you can make a simple, effective edging by twisting a thin fondant strand and laying it around the top or base of a cake (Fig. c). Use dabs of water to hold it in place.

Quilting and embossing
You can create a quilted effect by using a ruler to press lines into the fondant. You can also achieve an embossed effect by pressing things into the fondant. Specialty stores and online suppliers sell decorative stamps especially designed for this, but you can also use cutters to make a similar effect (see Hearts and Ribbons on pages 92–3).

C

Fondant cutters

There are all sorts of cutters available from specialty stores and online suppliers, which you can use to cut out a variety of patterns and shapes, including flowers and leaves.

The tiny cutters in the foreground of this photo below are called plunge cutters. They cut out tiny flower shapes. They have a small plunger inside that helps expel the flower so you can press it directly onto the cake.

Lettering

It is also possible to buy sets of alphabet cutters so you can cut out letters and stick words on the top of your cake. You can also use letter cutters as embossers and press them into the iced cake to make words.

A

B

Modeling with fondant

Simple figures

If you were to pull a fondant figure apart, you would see that the shapes of the components are very simple—usually a collection of cone, ball, and sausage shapes (Fig. a). Make the components as you go along; otherwise, the pieces may crack when you come to assemble the figure.

It is easier to make lying or sitting figures rather than standing ones. If the figure seems a bit wobbly, poke a short length of uncooked spaghetti inside to act as a support. Use light dabs of water to stick the components of the body together.

Plaques

There are a couple of advantages to using decorated plaques on a cake. First, they can be made weeks in advance. Second, if you are a little scared about piping a message directly on to a cake, you can pipe it onto a plaque first then place the plaque on the cake. If you make a mistake on a plaque, it takes only minutes to make another.

1. Cut out a piece of fondant to the desired shape. Let dry.

2. Decorate the plaque in whatever manner you like—it can be piped, painted on, or decorated with candies.

Simple roses

Cakes decorated with fondant flowers look beautiful, but they are quite tricky to make and take a lot of practice. However, simple roses are very easy to make and look effective and elegant (Fig. b). There is an even simpler rose shown on page 140 that can be made out of fondant as well.

1. Make a small fondant cone shape. Pinch one side to make a flap and wind around the outside of the cone.

2. Make two small, flat petals and stick around the center, on the lower part of the petal, with dabs of water.

3. Make three more petal shapes and stick around the outside of the rose. The petals should overlap slightly. Tweak the tips of the petals and cut off any excess from the base. Cut simple leaf shapes out of green fondant. Press the back of a knife into the fondant to create veins.

Templates

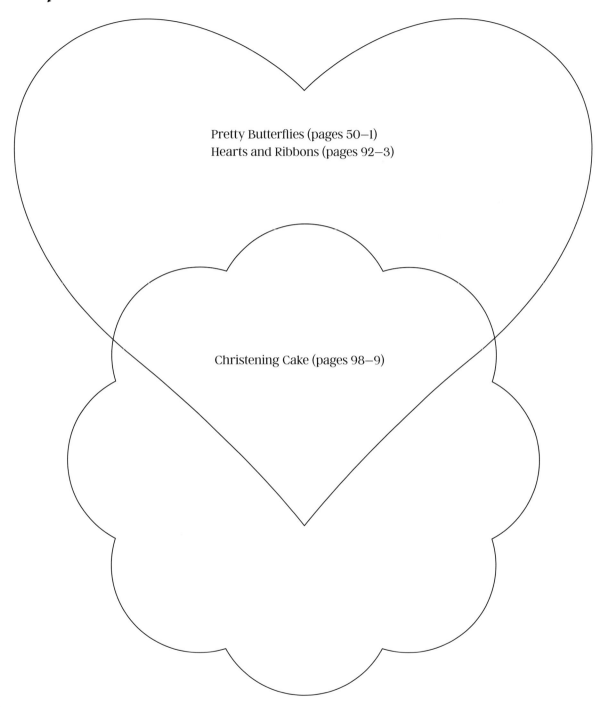

Pretty Butterflies (pages 50–1)
Hearts and Ribbons (pages 92–3)

Christening Cake (pages 98–9)

These templates are shown at 80 percent

Party Balloons

A versatile cake that is suitable for all sorts of happy occasions—birthdays, retirement parties, housewarmings, graduations—basically any special occasion.

INGREDIENTS

- 6 in. (15cm) round sponge cake (see page 13)
- 1 quantity buttercream frosting (see page 37)
- Confectioners' sugar, for rolling out
- 1 lb. 2 oz. (500g) white fondant
- 1 oz. (30g) red fondant
- 1 oz. (30g) yellow fondant
- 1 oz. (30g) blue fondant
- 1 oz. (30g) green fondant
- Black paste food coloring
- Small, round coated chocolate candies, such as M&M's

EQUIPMENT

- Carving knife
- Palette knife
- 8 in. (20cm) round cake board
- Rolling pin
- Cake smoother (optional)
- Small sharp knife
- Piping bag (see page 113, but read tip right first)
- No. 1 piping nozzle (see tip right)

TECHNIQUES

- Filling the cake (see page 38)
- Covering with buttercream (see page 38)
- Coloring fondant (see page 77)
- Covering a cake with fondant (see page 74)

1. Dust your work surface with confectioners' sugar and then knead and roll out the white fondant to a thickness of about ¾ in. (2cm).

2. Roll each of the four fondant colors into tiny balls and stick onto the white fondant, using very light dabs of water.

3. Roll over the entire slab of fondant (Fig. a). As they are pushed into the fondant, the balls should lengthen and form balloon shapes.

4. Lift and place the fondant over the cake. Smooth the top and sides and trim away any excess fondant from around the base.

5. Color about 1 Tbsp. of frosting black or dark gray and place into a piping bag fitted with a No. 1 piping nozzle. At the bottom of each balloon, pipe two triangles to give the impression of a bow and a wiggly string (Fig. b).

6. Using frosting, stick a line of colored candies around the base of the cake and place a few extra candies on the top.

· ·

Tip   If you don't want to pipe the strings on the balloons, you can paint them instead using black food coloring and a fine paintbrush.

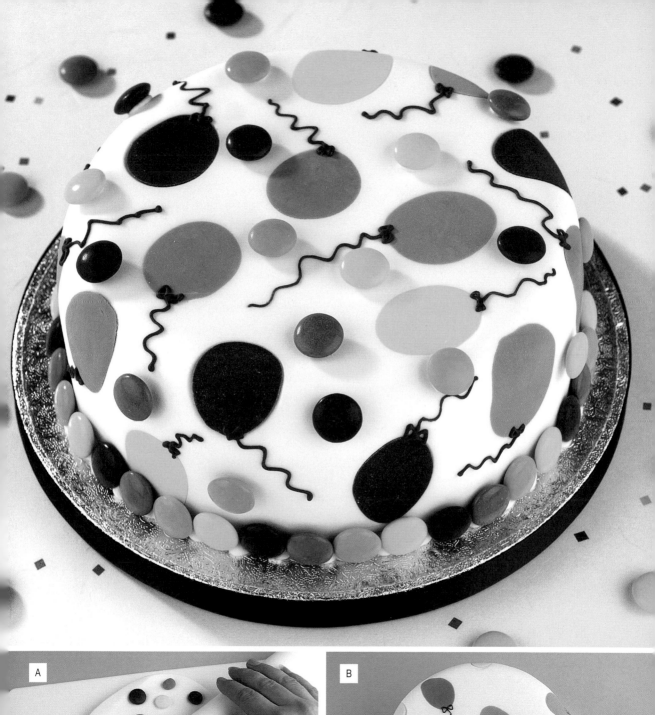

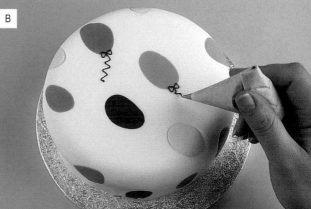

Fearsome Dragon

Will any daring knight or princess dare to steal the mini-cupcakes cakes this fearsome dragon is guarding? I think so! Because mini-cupcakes cakes are so simple to make and decorate, this is a project that even children could help with.

INGREDIENTS
- 1½ lbs. (750g) green fondant
- ½ oz. (15g) white fondant
- Confectioners' sugar, for rolling out
- Black paste food coloring or black food-coloring pen
- 6–7 square chocolate cookies
- About 12 decorated mini-cupcakes (see page 14)

EQUIPMENT
- Round dinner plate or cake board (approx. 12 in./30 cm)
- Piping nozzle (any)
- Small sharp knife
- Paintbrush

TECHNIQUES
- Coloring fondant (see page 77)
- Pudding bowl, layer, and mini-cupcakes cakes (see page 14)
- Quilting and embossing (see page 80)

Tips

Because the dragon is made of fondant, it can be made weeks in advance and kept in a box away from dust and daylight until required.

You can stand birthday cake candles along the dragon's spine. Alternatively, you can stand them in the mini-cupcakes. However, if you do this, don't light the candles until the cake is on the table and make sure there's no danger of one of the cupcakes slipping while the candles are lit.

1. Begin with the dragon's body. Roll out about 1¼ lbs. (600g) of green fondant into a tapering sausage shape about 25 in. (65cm) long (Fig. a).

2. Use dabs of water to stick the body in place around the outside edge of the plate.

3. Holding a piping nozzle at a slight angle, press it into the body to give the impression of scales (Fig. b).

4. Pull a lump off the leftover green fondant and put to one side to use later for the eyelids and ears. Roll the rest into a sausage shape for the head. Squeeze the middle so that it goes in and stick the head against the thickest part of the body. Add scales.

5. Use the back of a knife to press a line around the front of the head for a mouth and the end of a paintbrush to press two holes for the nostrils.

6. To make the eyes, make two tiny white fondant almond shapes. Stick them onto the face with water. Make two tiny green fondant string shapes for eyebrows and stick over the eyes.

7. Make two tiny green carrot shapes for ears and stick onto the head. Press a paintbrush handle into each one to give a bit of definition.

8. Paint two black dots on the eyes with black food coloring and a paintbrush or with a black food-coloring pen.

9. Cut about six square chocolate cookies in half diagonally and press into the dragon's back to make his spikes. Use one cookie to make the point on his tail.

10. Fill the center of the plate with decorated mini-cupcakes cakes.

Variation

The dinosaur to the right is made in exactly the same way as the dragon except that once the fondant has been rolled into a head shape, the back of the head is pulled and pinched to form a frill shape. It also doesn't have any spikes.

A

B

Frosted Flowers

A design so simple, there's virtually no decorating involved! You can frost other flowers such as freesias, pansies, petunias, primroses, and violets. If you choose flowers other than these, make sure that they are not poisonous. With deep red roses and a red or dark green ribbon, this would also make a stunning Christmas cake.

INGREDIENTS
- 8 in. (20 cm) round sponge cake (see page 13)
- 1 quantity buttercream frosting (see page 37)
- Confectioners' sugar, for rolling out
- 2 lb. (1kg) white or ivory fondant
- 1 egg white or ⅓ cup (75g/2½ oz.) superfine (caster) sugar dissolved in 1 Tbsp. hot, boiled water
- ½ cup (113g/4 oz.) superfine (caster) sugar

EQUIPMENT
- Carving knife
- Palette knife
- 10 in. (25cm) round cake board
- Rolling pin
- Cake smoother (optional)
- Small sharp knife
- Soft paintbrush
- 6–8 rose blooms (washed, dried, and stems cut off)
- Saucer
- 10–12 rose leaves (washed and dried)
- 28 in. (70cm) pink ribbon, 1½ in. (4cm) wide
- Clear tape

TECHNIQUES
- Filling the cake (see page 38)
- Covering with buttercream (see page 38)
- Covering a cake with fondant (see page 74)
- Covering cake boards with fondant (see pages 75–6)
- Ribbons (see page 34)

1. Level the top of the cake and turn it upside down so that the flat base now forms the top of the cake. Slice the cake horizontally into two or three layers; fill the layers with buttercream frosting and reassemble.

2. Place the cake on the cake board and spread a thin covering of frosting around the top and sides. Place to one side.

3. Dust your work surface with confectioners' sugar and knead the fondant until pliable. Roll it out and lift and place over the cake. Smooth the top and sides and trim away the excess from around the base.

4. Pick out any leftover fondant and use it to cover the cake board using the bandage method (see page 75).

5. Using a soft paintbrush, dab egg white or sugar solution around the tips of one of the rose blooms (Fig. a).

6. Dip the rose into a saucer of superfine sugar. Shake off the excess and let dry (Fig. b).

7. When they're dry, arrange the roses and leaves on top of the cake. Place the ribbon around the base of the cake. Cut to size and use a small piece of tape to secure it at the back.

Variation

This version uses silk flowers, so it's ideal for that last-minute cake panic.

Scary Halloween Cake

Marbling is an easy effect to achieve with fondant and the ghoulish, red-veined eyeballs are also simple to make. You should be able to find gummy snakes easily, but if you prefer to make your own, roll balls of fondant into snakes instead.

INGREDIENTS

- 6 in. (15cm) round sponge cake (see page 13)
- 1 quantity buttercream frosting (see page 37)
- 1 lb. 2oz. (500g) white fondant
- Confectioners' sugar, for rolling out
- 1 oz. (30g) black fondant
- Red paste food coloring
- 7–8 gummy snakes
- Black paste food coloring or black food-coloring pen

EQUIPMENT

- Carving knife
- Palette knife
- 10 in. (25cm) round cake board
- Rolling pin
- Cake smoother (optional)
- Small sharp knife
- Fine paintbrushes

TECHNIQUES

- Filling the cake (see page 38)
- Covering with buttercream (see page 38)
- Marbling (see page 78)
- Covering a cake with fondant (see page 74)
- Painting on fondant (see page 79)

1. Level the top of the cake and turn it upside down. Slice it two or three times horizontally and sandwich the layers together with buttercream frosting. Place the cake on the cake board and spread frosting around the sides and top.

2. Pull off a 3 oz. (90g) lump of white fondant and place to one side. Dust your work surface with confectioners' sugar and knead the remaining white fondant until soft.

3. Tear ¾ oz. (20g) of the black fondant into small pieces and press into the white. Roll the two colors into a thick sausage shape. Fold the sausage in half and re-roll. Repeat another two or three times, then roll out (Fig. a).

4. Lift and place the fondant on top of the cake and smooth the top and sides. Trim away any excess from around the base.

5. Pull a little bit off the white fondant you set aside at the beginning. Put this to one side for making highlights and snake eyes later. Roll the rest into three ball shapes for the eyeballs.

6. Divide the leftover black fondant into three and roll into three balls. Flatten the balls into disks and stick one onto each eye with a dab of water.

7. Make three tiny flat white disks and stick one onto each eye for highlights.

8. Paint blood vessels on to the eyes using red food coloring and a fine paintbrush (Fig. b). Stick the eyeballs in place on top of the cake with dabs of water.

9. Arrange the snakes around the top of the cake and the cake board. If they won't stay in place, stick them with little dabs of water.

10. Make two tiny white fondant balls for eyes for each snake and stick on with water. Using either black food coloring and a fine paintbrush or a black food-coloring pen, add tiny black dots for pupils.

Tip ·········

For a really ghoulish surprise, you could color the cake mixture green before baking and fill it with orange or purple buttercream frosting.

A

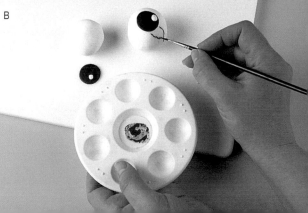

B

Hearts and Ribbons

This cake is a festive idea for Valentine's Day or an anniversary. Ribbon insertion is a traditional form of cake decorating. Here, the wide ribbon gives the cake a more contemporary feel. A variation of this cake is shown on page 73.

INGREDIENTS
- 7 in. (18cm) square sponge cake (see page 13)
- 1 quantity buttercream frosting (see page 37)
- Confectioners' sugar, for rolling out
- 1½ lbs. (750g) white fondant
- 6½ oz. (200g) red fondant
- 2 Tbsp. white royal icing (optional; see page 106 or tip opposite)

EQUIPMENT
- Waxed or tracing paper
- Pencil
- Scissors
- Carving knife
- Palette knife
- 10 in. (25cm) round cake board
- Rolling pin
- Cake smoother (optional)
- Small sharp knife
- Heart-shaped cutter
- Piping bag (see page 113)
- No. 3 piping nozzle (optional; see tip opposite)
- Scalpel or small, sharp knife
- 1 yd. (1m) ribbon
- Paintbrush

TECHNIQUES
- Filling the cake (see page 38)
- Covering with buttercream (see page 38)
- Covering a cake with fondant (see page 74)
- Quilting and embossing (see page 80)
- Covering cake boards with fondant (see page 75–6)
- Piping (see page 112–9)

1. Trace the heart template on page 83 and cut out. Place the template on the cake and cut around it (see Fig. b on page 51).

2. Split the cake into two or three layers and reassemble it, sandwiching the layers together with buttercream frosting. Place the cake on the cake board. Spread a thin coating of frosting over the sides and top of the cake.

3. Dust your work surface with confectioners' sugar and roll out the white fondant to a thickness of about a ½ in. (1cm). Lift and place it onto the cake and smooth the fondant into position. Trim away the excess from around the base.

4. Gently press a heart-shaped cutter into the fondant to leave an impression of the shape (Fig. a). Try not to go right through the fondant or there's a chance the frosting might ooze out. Repeat all over the cake.

5. Moisten the exposed cake board with a little water. Thinly roll out the red fondant. Cut it into strips and lay it around the base of the cake so that it covers the cake board. Trim the edges so they are neat (Fig. b).

6. Place about 1 Tbsp. of white royal icing into a piping bag fitted with a No. 3 piping nozzle and pipe a "snail trail" (see page 116) around the base of the cake.

7. Using a scalpel or an extremely sharp knife, cut two slits the same length as the width of your ribbon about 1 in. (2.5cm) apart on the side of the cake.

8. Cut about 2 in. (5cm) of ribbon. Insert the ends into the slits (Fig. c). Use the scalpel to poke the ribbon in securely. Repeat two or three times over the cake.

9. Make a bow with the remaining ribbon and stick on top of the cake using either a dab of royal icing or a moistened ball of white fondant.

10. Brush away any dusty fingerprints from the cake board with a soft, damp paintbrush.

Tip ·········

Don't want to pipe around the base of the cake? Stick small white fondant balls around it instead. Because of the amount of fabric on this design, it is not advisable to use candles.

A

B

C

Christmas Gift

The technique shown here is a simple pattern. Fondant shapes are cut out and replaced with others of an identical shape but in a different color. You don't have to use fruitcake with this design. Instead, substitute with sponge cake and buttercream frosting and omit the marzipan if you prefer.

INGREDIENTS
- 6 in. (15cm) square fruitcake (see pages 20–2)
- 3 Tbsp. brandy (optional)
- 3 Tbsp. boiled apricot jam
- Confectioners' sugar, for rolling out
- 1 lb. 2 oz. (500g) marzipan (see page 100)
- 1 lb. 2 oz. (500g) white fondant
- 8 oz. (250g) green fondant
- 1½ oz. (45g) red fondant

EQUIPMENT
- Carving knife
- 8 in. (20cm) square cake board
- Toothpick
- Pastry brush
- Rolling pin
- Cake smoother (optional)
- Small sharp knife
- Holly leaf cutter
- 1 yd. (1m) ribbon
- Scissors

TECHNIQUES
- Covering a fruitcake for fondant or swirled royal icing (see page 101)
- Covering a cake with fondant (see page 74)

1. Level the top of the cake and turn it upside down on the cake board. Pierce the top of the cake a few times with the toothpick and drizzle the brandy over the top. Brush the apricot jam over the top and sides of the cake.

2. Dust your work surface with confectioners' sugar. Knead and roll out the marzipan. Lay the marzipan over the top of the cake and smooth the top and sides. Trim any excess from around the base.

3. Place a few light dabs of water on the surface of the marzipan. These are just to hold the fondant covering in place. If you soak the marzipan, you will not be able to remove the fondant cutouts, so use a light hand.

4. Sprinkle more confectioners' sugar on your work surface and knead and roll out the white fondant. Lift and place over the cake. Smooth the top and trim the edges so they are neat.

5. Press the holly leaf cutter into the cake. Try to just cut through the fondant and not the marzipan or the cake. Remove the leaf shape (Fig. a). Cut out leaf shapes all over the cake.

6. Roll out the green fondant. Try to make it roughly the same thickness as the white fondant cake covering.

7. Using the holly leaf cutter, cut out enough green leaves to replace the white ones you have cut out of the cake. Re-roll the leftover green fondant as necessary.

8. Place the leaves into the gaps on the cake using dabs of water (Fig. b). Using the back of a knife, press a few lines into each leaf for veins.

9. Make tiny red fondant balls for berries. Squash them and stick on to the cake with water.

10. To tie the ribbon, pass both ends under the cake board and tie in a knot. Bring the ends back up and tie into a bow. Trim the ends if necessary so they are neat.

Tips

By using different cutters, you could easily adapt this design to suit any occasion. For example, use a flower cutter and pink fondant to make a pretty birthday gift.

If you wanted to personalize the design, you could make a rectangular fondant label and pipe a message onto it.

Happy Gardener

Although brown sugar makes incredibly realistic looking soil, it is very crunchy. If you prefer a softer alternative, dab chocolate buttercream frosting around the top and base of the cake instead.

INGREDIENTS

- 8 in. (20cm) square sponge cake (see page 13)
- 1 quantity buttercream frosting (see page 37)
- Confectioners' sugar, for rolling out
- 1 lb. 12 oz. (800g) cream-colored fondant
- 2½ oz. (75g) brown fondant
- Black food coloring
- 11 oz. (300g) green fondant
- 1 strand uncooked spaghetti
- 4 oz. (100g) flesh-/terracotta-colored fondant (use "paprika" paste food coloring or a mixture of pink, yellow, and white fondant)
- Silver food coloring (optional; see tip)
- 1½ oz. (45g) dark brown sugar

EQUIPMENT

- Carving knife
- Palette knife
- 10 in. (25cm) square cake board
- Rolling pin
- Cake smoother (optional)
- Small, sharp knife
- Paintbrush
- Piping nozzle (any)

1. Level the top of the cake and turn it over so that the base now forms the top. Slice the cake horizontally into two or three layers and then sandwich the layers back together with buttercream frosting. Place the cake onto the board and thinly coat the sides and top of the cake with frosting.

2. Dust your work surface with confectioners' sugar. Knead the cream-colored fondant until pliable and roll it out to a thickness of about ⅓ in. (1cm). Lift and place over the cake. Smooth the top and sides and trim away the excess with a sharp knife.

3. To make the gardener, roll 2 oz. (60g) of brown fondant into a sausage shape, 7 in. (18cm) long. Bend it into a horseshoe shape (Fig. a). Slice the ends off and stick in the center of the cake with a dab of water.

4. Knead a little black food coloring into about 5 oz. (150g) of green fondant to make a khaki color. Roll about 3 oz. (90g) into a conical shape for his body. Flatten the base and top slightly and stick on top of the legs with a little water.

5. To stop the gardener from falling over, stick a strand of spaghetti into the body. Leave a bit protruding for the head.

6. Roll about 1 oz. (30g) flesh-colored fondant into a ball for the man's head. Stick it on top of the body (Fig. b). Poke the edge of a piping nozzle into the lower part of the face to make a smile.

7. Make three tiny flesh-colored ball shapes. Use these for the ears and nose and stick them in position. Poke a hollow into each ear with the end of a paintbrush.

8. Roll ⅓ oz. (10g) of the khaki fondant into a ball and flatten it to make the cap. Stick the cap on top of his head and press a line into the front of the cap with the back of a knife.

9. Roll about ¾ oz. (20g) of the khaki fondant into a sausage. Cut it in half to make his arms. Stick one on either side of his body.

10. For the boots, make two ½ oz. (15g) khaki sausages. Bend into "L" shapes and stick on to the legs. Press four lines into the sole of each boot with the back of a knife.

11. To make a flowerpot, roll ½ oz. (15g) of the flesh-colored fondant into a conical shape. Flatten the base and top. Roll and cut out a long thin flesh-colored strip and stick around the top of the pot (Fig. c). Make three pots and stick around the man. Paint a dot using black food coloring on the base of each pot.

12. Make two fondant balls for the gardener's hands; flatten slightly. Stick one on the end of each arm, resting one arm on the top of a flowerpot.

13. To make a spade, roll ⅓ oz. (10g) of the brown fondant into a long string. Cut a small section off the end and lay across the top of the longer section to form a "T" shape. Stick onto the cake and add a square cream piece of fondant for the blade.

14. For the trowel, roll a tiny bit of brown fondant into a pellet shape for the handle. Make a similar cream shape for the blade. Press a paintbrush handle into the blade to give it a curved shape. Stick onto the cake.

15. Paint the relevant parts of the trowel and spade with silver food coloring.

16. Use the remaining green fondant to make the leaves. Roll it out thinly and cut out simple leaf shapes. Press a couple of veins into each leaf with the back of a knife, put a dab of water on the back of each leaf and stick them around the sides of the cake.

17. To finish, moisten the top of the cake with a little water and carefully spoon the sugar around the character. Do the same around the leaves on the cake board.

Tip ·

If you cannot find silver food coloring, use gray fondant to make the trowel and spade blades instead.

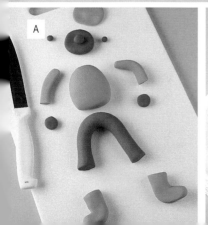

A

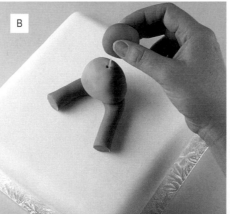

B

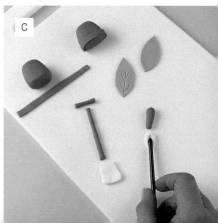

C

Christening Cake

At first glance, this may look like a terribly complicated cake to attempt, but it isn't as tricky as it looks. You can take your time with it. The top plaque with the bootees can be made weeks in advance. The pretty technique here, broderie anglaise, mimics eyelet needlework, and it works just as well in blue (see Baby's Cradle on pages 128–9).

INGREDIENTS
- 8 in. (20cm) square sponge cake (see page 13)
- 1 quantity buttercream frosting (see page 37)
- Confectioners' sugar, for rolling out
- 2 lb. 4 oz. (1kg) white fondant
- 1 lb. 2 oz. (500g) pink fondant
- 1 quantity royal icing (see page 106)
- Pink paste food coloring

EQUIPMENT
- Carving knife
- Palette knife
- 12 in. (30cm) square cake board
- Rolling pin
- Cake smoother (optional)
- Small, sharp knife
- Paintbrush
- Piping bags (see page 113)
- Star piping nozzle
- Waxed or tracing paper
- Pencil
- Scissors
- No. 1 piping nozzle
- 1 yd. (1m) thin, pink ribbon

TECHNIQUES
- Filling the cake (see page 38)
- Covering with buttercream (see page 38)
- Covering a cake with fondant (see page 74)
- Covering cake boards with fondant (see pages 75–6)
- Piping (see pages 112–9)

1. To prepare the cake, level the top and turn it upside down. Slice it horizontally into two or three layers, fill with buttercream frosting, and reassemble. Place it in the center of the cake board and spread frosting around the sides and top.

2. Dust your work surface with confectioners' sugar and knead and roll out 1 lb. 10 oz. (800g) of the white fondant. Lift and place over the cake. Smooth the top and sides and trim the edges around the base so they are neat.

3. Lightly moisten the visible cake board and thinly roll out about 12 oz. (350g) of the pink fondant. Cut into four strips and use it to cover the cake board (see page 76). Trim the edges so they are neat.

4. Using a paintbrush handle, press a series of dots and dashes into the pink fondant to form a pattern. The center of a flower is a dot, and a series of six dashes around the outside form the petals (refer to Fig. a). Place about 3 Tbsp. of white royal icing into a piping bag fitted with a star nozzle and pipe a "snail trail" around the base of the cake.

5. To make the plaque, roll out another 5 oz. (150g) of the pink fondant. Trace the template on page 83 and cut it out. Place the template onto the pink fondant and cut out the flower shape. Using the paintbrush, press a line of dots around the outside of the shape and a circle of dot and dash flowers just inside (Fig. a).

6. Place about 1 Tbsp. of white royal icing into a piping bag fitted with a No. 1 piping nozzle. Carefully pipe around the outside of all the dots and dashes on both the board and the plaque (Fig. b).

7. Place a few dabs of water on top of the cake. Using a palette knife, carefully lift and place the plaque into position.

8. To make the bootees, make two ½ oz. (15g) white fondant balls. Squash both into flattish oval shapes. Take another two ½ oz. (15g) lumps of white fondant and roll out. Cut out two

98 CHRISTENING CAKE

rectangles about 5 in. (12cm) long. Round the corners of the rectangles slightly.

9. Fold a rectangle around the top of an oval to form a bootee (Fig. c). Poke a few lace holes with the end of a paintbrush. Repeat with the second bootee then stick them in place on the plaque with a light dab of water.

10. Color about 2 Tbsp. of royal icing pink and place in a piping bag with a No. 1 piping nozzle.

11. Pipe a couple of lines on each bootee to make the laces.

11. Pipe a zigzag pattern around the edges of the plaque to hide any rough edges.

12. Pipe a small floral pattern on each of the four corners of the cake using a series of dots and dashes.

13. Make four tiny pink ribbon bows and stick in position with dots of royal icing.

Tip When using a fine piping nozzle, it helps if you make the frosting slightly runnier than usual by stirring in a few drops of water.

Variation · · · · · · ·

A plaque this shape suits all sorts of other shaped cakes as well. Here the plaque has been decorated more intricately. You could pipe the baby's name in the center if you wish.

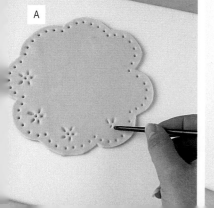

A

B

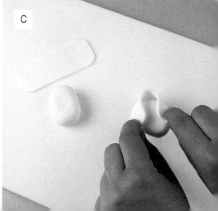

C

MARZIPAN

Made out of ground almonds, the difference between marzipan and almond paste is that marzipan contains a higher proportion of almonds, so it's usually a little more expensive. The taste is very similar, and they behave the same way when working with them. You can make your own marzipan or you can buy it. It is readily available from online suppliers or specialty stores in two shades: the traditional yellow (labeled "gold") or white. It can be colored using food coloring, so it could be used instead of fondant for most of the designs on pages 84—99. For best results, it is advised that you cover your cakes with marzipan before applying fondant or royal icing.

Recipe

This recipe lightly cooks the eggs and produces a marzipan that is fairly firm and not too oily. (If you are concerned about the eggs being only lightly cooked, see page 5; you may choose to use ready-made marzipan instead.)

INGREDIENTS

· 1 whole egg and 1 egg yolk
· 4 oz. (110g) superfine (caster) sugar
· 4 oz. (110g) confectioners' sugar (sifted)
· A few drops of almond extract
· 8 oz. (225g) ground almonds

1. Put the whole egg, egg yolk, superfine sugar, and confectioners' sugar into a heatproof bowl and place over a pan of hot water. Whisk until thick and creamy.

2. Remove the bowl from the heat and add a few drops of almond extract. Using a wooden spoon, stir in the ground almonds then lightly knead into a ball. The marzipan will firm up slightly as it cools, but if you feel it is still too soft, add a little more confectioners' sugar.

Storing: Ideally marzipan should be used as soon as possible, but if you have to store it for a day or so, double-wrap it in a small plastic bag or plastic wrap and keep it in the refrigerator. Use within a week.

Tip: If the marzipan is hard to knead, microwave it for 10 to 15 seconds. Test it and repeat if necessary. Don't overdo it because the oils in the center can burn.

Above: Marzipan shapes are quick and easy to make.

QUANTITY GUIDE

Although amounts will vary depending on how thick you like your marzipan, here is a rough guide to the quantities you will require to cover different sizes of cakes.

Round cake	6 in. (15cm)	7 in. (18cm)	8 in. (20cm)	9 in. (23cm)	10 in. (25cm)	11 in. (28cm)	12 in. (30cm)	—
Square cake	—	6 in. (15cm)	7 in. (18cm)	8 in. (20cm)	9 in. (23cm)	10 in. (25cm)	11 in. (28cm)	12 in. (30cm)
Amount of marzipan	1 lb. 2 oz. (500g)	1 lb. 5 oz. (650g)	1 lb. 10 oz. (800g)	2 lbs. (900g)	2½ lbs. (1.1kg)	3 lbs. (1.4kg)	3½ lbs. (1.6kg)	4 lbs. (1.8kg)

Covering a fruitcake for fondant or swirled royal icing

Because razor sharp edges are not required for fondant or swirled royal icing, the whole cake can be covered all at one time.

1. Place the cake in position on the cake board. If the top is slightly domed, slice this off and place the cake upside down on the board. Fill any holes with small balls of marzipan. If you wish, drizzle a little brandy over the top of the cake and allow it to sink in. Heat some apricot jam in a small saucepan or in a bowl in the microwave to boiling point and brush over the top and sides of the cake. Knead the marzipan. Dust your work surface with confectioners' sugar and roll it out (Fig. a).

2. Carefully lift the marzipan and place it on the cake (Fig. b).

3. Ease it over the top and sides of the cake and gently press into position. Trim away any excess from around the base (Fig. c).

4. Smooth over the top and sides with the flat of your hands. Ideally, then use a cake smoother (Fig. d).

A

B

C

D

A

B

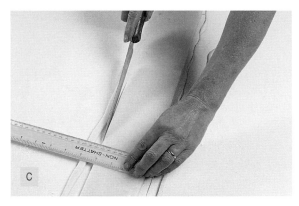

C

D

Covering a round fruitcake for smooth royal icing

1. If the top of the cake is rounded, level it so that it is flat and turn the cake over. Fill any holes with small balls of marzipan. Drizzle a little brandy over the cake if you wish and allow it to sink in. Heat some apricot jam in a small saucepan or in a bowl in the microwave to boiling point and brush over the top of the cake (Fig. a).

2. Knead about two thirds of the marzipan and roll it out to no less than ¼ in. (5mm) thickness. Place the cake upside down on the marzipan and cut around the edge (Fig. b).

3. Turn the cake right side up and place on the cake board. Measure the circumference of the cake and make a note of the measurement. Spread the jam around the sides. Knead and roll out the rest of the marzipan (including the trimmings). Cut a strip the same length as the circumference of the cake and as wide as the height of the cake, including the marzipan topping (Fig. c).

4. Roll the marzipan strip up like a bandage and unwind it around the sides of the cake (Fig. d).

5. Let dry for at least 48 hours before icing. It is important that the surfaces, edges, and corners of the marzipan are smooth and sharp, since any crinkle or bump will show through the royal icing.

Covering a square fruitcake for smooth royal icing

1. Level the top of the cake if necessary and brush it with boiled apricot jam (Fig. a).

2. Knead about two thirds of the marzipan and roll it out to no less than ¼ in. (5mm) thickness. Place the cake, upside down on the marzipan. Trim around the cake (Fig. b) and place right side up on the board.

3. Measure the length and width of one side of the cake. Cut four strips of marzipan using those measurements (Fig. c).

4. Spread the jam over the sides and stick the strips of marzipan onto the cake (Fig. d).

5. Let the cake dry for at least 48 hours before icing. Make sure that all of the surfaces, edges, and corners are as smooth and sharp as possible.

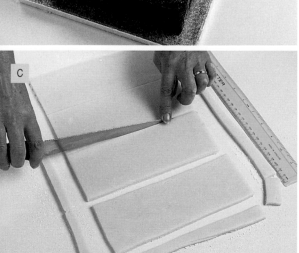

Coloring marzipan

It is easy to color marzipan. Simply add color (paste or gel colors work best since they're less likely to make the marzipan soggy) and knead in. Because gold marzipan is already quite a strong color, it will distort some colors, such as blue, and give them a greenish tint. Therefore, if you're planning to color marzipan, it's best to use the white variety.

1. Apply the color to the marzipan with a toothpick (Fig. a).

2. Knead the color into the marzipan, ensuring that it is evenly blended (Fig. b).

A

B

Modeling with marzipan

The principles of modeling with marzipan are the same as those for fondant (see page 82). You can make models of virtually anything—people, animals, flowers, and so on. Use water to stick the pieces of marzipan together.

Little fruit like these are fun and easy to make. They could be used as cake decorations or even as sweet treats at Christmas. The blush on the apple was made by brushing a little edible dusting powder over the green. You could achieve a similar effect by dabbing a little red food coloring on the apple instead.

Above: On this design, nuts were arranged on top of the fruitcake before baking, then glazed with boiled apricot jam when the cake had cooled. A pattern of simple marzipan Santas stands around the edges. You could use stars if you prefer.

Using marzipan fruit is a very simple way to create a beautifully decorated cake. The edge is simply crimped (see page 80) and the cake and board trimmed with a yellow ribbon.

ROYAL ICING

Royal icing is extremely versatile. Made from egg whites and confectioners' sugar, it can be used for both covering and piping cakes. It has a more crisp texture than fondant and gives a cake a very classic, polished look. Because it sets hard, it can be used to create all sorts of extravagant effects. When using royal icing, it is important that all of your bowls and utensils are dry and grease-free, so wash them in hot, soapy water before you start. It may take a few attempts to perfect your technique with royal icing, but the finished result is worth the effort.

Recipe

If you are using royal icing to coat a cake, it is essential that you include glycerin and lemon juice. The glycerin enables you to get a knife cleanly through the icing when you cut the cake, and the lemon juice keeps the icing white.

   If you are just making icing to pipe flowers, make a "snail trail" around a cake or to make the run-outs on the Snowflakes (see pages 132–3) and Baby's Cradle (see pages 128–9) cakes, you can leave these two items out.

   There is a slight risk of salmonella from using raw eggs (see note on page 5). If you prefer, you can used dried egg white substitute; refer to the instructions on the package. Also, it is suggested that you use an electric mixer for this recipe, rather than manually mixing the ingredients. An electric mixer makes the recipe much easier to complete.

INGREDIENTS
(Amounts for 1 quantity)
- 2 egg whites (or equivalent amount of dried egg white, reconstituted)
- 1 lb. 2 oz. (500g) confectioners' sugar, sifted
- 1 tsp. (5ml) lemon juice
- 1 tsp. (5ml) glycerin

1. Add egg whites to the mixing bowl and beat well until light and frothy.

2. Stir in about a quarter of the confectioners' sugar. If using a mixer, set it to the slowest speed.

3. Gradually add the rest of the sugar, the lemon juice, and glycerin.

4. Beat until the icing stands up in peaks. If you're using a mixer, beat on slow speed for 5 minutes. Don't be tempted to race ahead on a fast speed or your icing will be too full of air bubbles to use properly.

Storing: When the icing is ready, transfer to a clean, grease-free plastic food container with a tight-fitting lid. Lay a sheet of plastic wrap directly on top of the icing to prevent it from drying out and place the lid back on the container. Always keep the icing covered when not in use and use within a week.

Using: If you have stored the icing, you will need to remix it before using. Take a few tablespoons of icing out of the container and place it in a small bowl. Beat it thoroughly with a knife to get rid of air bubbles and to make it nice and smooth. Repeat if necessary. If you want to stop the leftover beaten icing from hardening, place a damp cloth over the top of the bowl.

A

B

Quantity guide

It is difficult to give even a rough guide for royal icing since it really depends on how thick you want your covering of icing to be. If you have a lot of cakes to cover, it is best to double the amount shown in the recipe and use that up before making another batch.

C

D

Coloring royal icing

It is possible to use either liquid or paste food coloring. If using liquid food coloring, don't add too much since you could over-thin the icing and make it too runny to hold its shape when piping. If you are trying to achieve a pale color, note that the icing will darken slightly as it dries.

1. Add the color sparingly to the icing (Fig. a).

2. Mix until the color in the icing is even throughout (Fig. b). If you want to keep any excess icing on hand in case you need more, lay a damp cloth over the top of the bowl.

Creating peaked and swirled effects

These are the easiest finishes to achieve on a royal iced cake since you don't have to be precise at all.

To get peaks in the icing, simply spread royal icing over the cake, press the palette knife into the icing and pull away sharply to leave a peak (Fig. c).

A swirly effect is achieved by simply swirling the icing about the cake as you cover it (Fig. d). This effect was used on Christmas Bows (see above and on pages 122–3).

A

B

C

D

Royal-icing a square fruitcake

This technique is used only on a fruitcake that has been covered with marzipan, never on a sponge cake. You will need a straightedge, which is like a metal ruler but has no markings on it, and a cake scraper to produce a smooth finish. It will take about a week to coat the cake because the icing has to dry between layers.

1. Spread some icing over the top of the cake with a palette knife. Spread it back and forth a few times to get rid of any air bubbles then spread it over the entire top of the cake. Cover the surface as evenly as possible (Fig. a).

2. Remove any excess icing from around the edges (Fig. b).

3. Take the straightedge and place it at the far end of the cake. Pull it toward you in one continuous movement (Fig. c). You should be left with a thin covering over the cake.

4. Remove any excess icing from around the edges (Fig. d) and allow the cake to dry for a minimum of 3 hours, preferably overnight.

5. Spread icing over one side of the cake (Fig. e).

6. Remove any excess icing from the top edge and the corners (Fig. f).

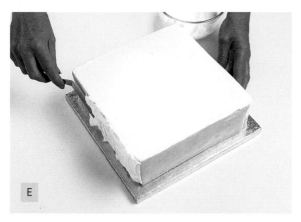

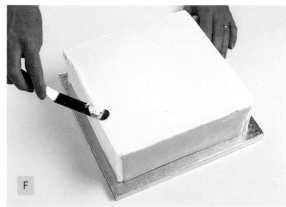

7. Stand the cake scraper at the far end of the cake and pull it toward you in one movement (Fig. g).

8. Remove any excess icing from the top edge and corners again (Fig. h). Allow the cake to dry for another couple of hours.

9. Cover the other sides in the same way then let the cake dry overnight (Fig. i).

10. Ice the cake with another two layers, allowing drying time between coats.

Covering a square cake board

Make sure that the royal iced cake is completely dry before putting it on a board; otherwise, you may damage its finish.

1. Spread a thin layer of royal icing over one side of the board. Remove any excess icing from the edge (Fig. a).

2. Pull the cake scraper over the icing toward you in one movement (Fig. b).

3. Remove any excess from the edges (Fig. c) and repeat on the opposite side. Allow the cake to dry for at least 3 hours and cover the other two sides. Repeat with a second layer for a neat finish.

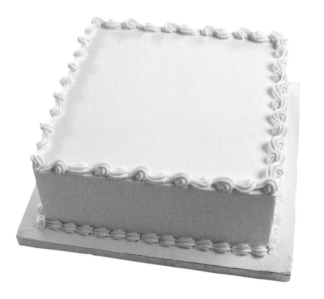

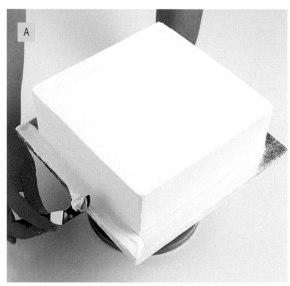

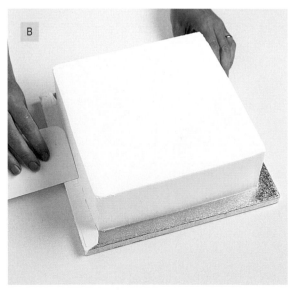

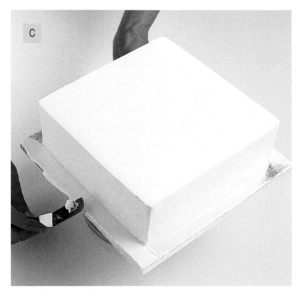

Royal-icing a round fruitcake

As well as a straightedge and cake scraper, you will need an icing turntable. This technique is used only on a fruitcake that has been covered with marzipan, never on a sponge cake. You need to allow a week to do this, since the icing has to dry between layers.

1. Cover the top surface of the cake in the same way as described for the square cake (see pages 108-9) and allow it to dry overnight (Fig. a).

2. Spread royal icing around the sides of the cake (Fig. b).

3. Remove any excess icing from around the top edge with a palette knife (Fig. c).

4. Place the cake on the turntable. Hold the cake scraper vertically at the back of the cake; hold the cake board and turntable with your other hand. Turn the turntable in one revolution,

pulling the scraper toward you (Fig. d). Lift the scraper off the cake (this will leave a mark).

5. Smooth the top edge again to make it neat (Fig. e). Allow the cake to dry overnight. Repeat the process, building up at least three layers.

A

B

C

Covering a round cake board

1. Stand the cake on a turntable. Spread a thin, even layer of royal icing around the board (Fig. a).

2. Remove any excess from the edges using a palette knife (Fig. b).

3. Run the cake scraper around the cake board in one continuous fluid motion (Fig. c).

4. Remove any excess from the edges again (Fig. d) and let dry for at least 3 hours. Repeat with a second coat.

D

Piping

The thought of piping can be a bit terrifying; however, if you have the right equipment and a bit of time to practice, anyone can learn some simple techniques.

There are a number of different piping options available, from shiny syringe-type contraptions to humble pieces of folded waxed paper. It is even possible to buy tubes of ready-made piping icing that come with a set of different screw-on nozzles. There is no right or wrong piece of equipment, so use whatever suits you.

Piping bags

Washable polyester piping bags: Using these bags has certain advantages. Obviously, because they're washable, they're reusable. They don't split and burst at inopportune moments and grease from buttercream doesn't seep through the sides. They are used with a connector to which you attach the piping nozzle. This means you can change the piping nozzle without having to set up a new bag. They're also handy for making meringues.

Disposable purchased bags: These bags are very convenient since they're already made up for you. There's no need to wash them after you've finished icing; you can just throw them away. Their only disadvantage is their cost.

Disposable homemade bags: This is definitely the cheapest option, since you can make hundreds of piping bags from one roll of waxed paper. These bags are quite easy to make (see instructions on the following page).

Above: This pretty cradle is made entirely out of piped royal icing (see pp. 108–9)

Piping equipment can be as simple and inexpensive as a homemade piping bag or as easy as store-bought tubes of ready-made icing.

Making a piping bag

1. Cut some waxed paper into a triangle.

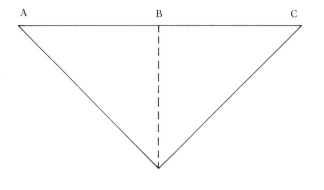

2. Pick up corner C and fold over, so that B forms a sharp cone in the center.

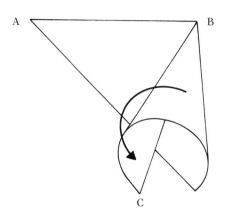

3. Wrap corner A around the cone.

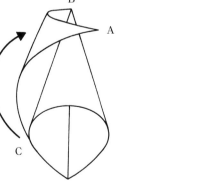

4. Make sure that A and C are at the back and that the point of the cone is sharp.

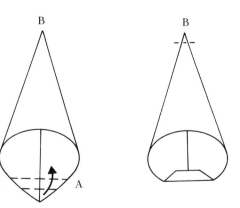

5. Fold points A and C inside the top edge of the bag to hold it securely. Snip off the end B and insert a nozzle.

Filling a piping bag

Usually you pipe with a piping nozzle in the end of the bag. If using a disposable or waxed paper bag, snip about ½ in. (12mm) off the end of the bag and drop a piping nozzle inside.

1. Scoop up some icing on a palette knife and place it inside the bag. Holding the knife through the bag, pull the knife out (Fig. a).

2. To close the bag fold the end over a couple of times and force the icing down into the nozzle (Fig. b).

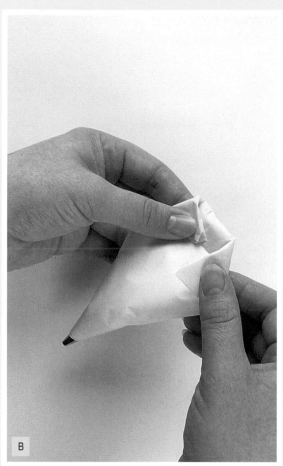

Creating different piping effects

There are many different types of piping nozzles available that enable you to create all sorts of wondrous patterns and effects. Many are made in plastic as well as metal. The difference (apart from the price) is that metal nozzles have slightly more accurate edges and create a sharper effect; they also tend to last a little longer.

Piping is just a question of pressure. You squeeze the bag, and the icing comes out. Release the pressure, and it stops. It really is that simple. That's not to say that you won't have the odd mishap here and there, but most mistakes are easy to fix or disguise. After a very short time, you'll be amazed at what you can do.

Check out a few of the most common nozzles and the effects you can achieve with them (page 116, Fig. a from top to bottom).

No. 2 This nozzle has a simple round hole at its tip. It's ideal for piping thin lines, writing, piping dots, and creating tiny "snail trails" around the edges of things. It is also easy to use a nozzle like this to make a simple floral pattern composed of dots and dashes.

No. 4 This nozzle has a bigger hole in the end than the No. 2, so it can be used for more dramatic effects. You can pipe dots, dashes, and even big flowers such as the ones on the Summer Flowers cake on pages 60–1.

Star As its name suggests, the serrated edges of this nozzle are ideal for piping star shapes. You can pipe single stars or even cover a whole cake (see Buttercream Flowers on pages 54–5). You can also use a nozzle like this to pipe a line of shells around the edges or base of a cake. See the instructions for "snail trail" below.

Petal Shaped a bit like a teardrop, this nozzle is ideal for piping flowers.

Leaf This very useful nozzle enables you to pipe leaf shapes quickly and easily. Wiggle the bag slightly as you pull it away, and you will end up with a lovely serrated effect.

Snail trail (See the top three examples in Fig. a.) This is a common technique used for piping around the base or edges of cakes. Using a nozzle with a plain or star-shaped tip, you squeeze a little icing out of the nozzle, release the pressure and pull along slightly so the icing tapers into a slight point. Keeping the nozzle still in the icing, squeeze another blob out and repeat.

Piping without a nozzle

You can pipe with a bag alone. However, you must use this bag right away before the end becomes soggy and distorted or the icing sets and blocks it. Fill and close the bag before cutting anything off the end.

Snip a "V" shape into the end of the bag This produces piping that has an interesting ridge along its back (top example in Fig. b).

Snip the end of the bag into a point You can make leaf shapes. Squeeze a little icing out of the end and release the pressure. Pull the bag away so that the icing tapers away into a tail (middle example in Fig. b).

Snip straight across the end of the bag, removing a tiny triangle Use this bag as you would a No. 2 piping nozzle. The larger the triangle you cut off the end, the thicker the line the bag will produce (bottom example in Fig. b).

Multicolored piping

On page 39 there is a demonstration, using buttercream frosting, of how you can place more than one color in a piping bag at a time. It is possible to do this with royal icing, too.

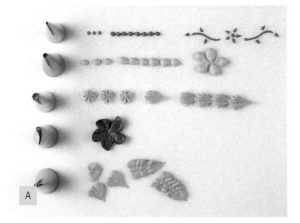

A

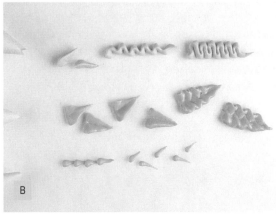

B

Piping flowers

Piping a simple five-petal blossom is a worthwhile technique to try to master since it means that as well as blossoms; you can also pipe violets and primroses. To make violets, color the icing purple and for primroses, color it yellow (see page 107). You will need an icing nail (which looks like a big woodworking nail) or a mini-turntable, which you can revolve in your fingers. Alternatively, you could use a piece of cork stuck on the end of a long nail.

C

1. Place the petal nozzle into a piping bag with about 2 tablespoons of colored icing. Fold over the end of the bag to close it.

2. Stick a square of waxed paper onto the top of the piping nail with a dab of icing.

3. With the thick end of the piping nozzle in the center of the flower, squeeze the bag and turn the nail. Slightly lift the thin edge of the nozzle as you turn, to form a petal. Release the pressure and pull away.

4. Wipe the end of the nozzle. Tuck the nozzle just underneath the edge of the first petal and pipe a second. Repeat, making five petals in total (Fig. c). Remove from the nail or turntable and let it dry on the paper. Add a yellow dot in the center to finish (Fig. d, top).

D

Daisy Pipe white lines fanning out in a circle and pipe a dot of yellow in the center (Fig. d, second row).

Hyacinth Pipe a central green stem then, using a star nozzle, pipe a few stars on either side (Fig. d, third row).

Piping lettering

There are various ways to position and pipe your message on top of a cake. This technique requires practice since you have to get used to writing with icing instead of a pen. You will develop your own style of "piping writing" and will know instinctively how much space you will need for your message.

Scribing A relatively simple way to transfer your message onto a cake covered in fondant or royal icing is by scribing. The cake should have been left to stand overnight so the surface has hardened.

Write your message on a piece of waxed paper and place it into position on the cake. Using a scribing tool (a bit like a paintbrush handle with a sharp point on the end) or a dressmaker's pin, trace over the lettering. When you remove the waxed paper, you should be able to see your message faintly scratched on the cake's surface. Use this as a guide to pipe over.

Freehand This is what you are ultimately aiming for: to be able to write freehand on your cakes. However, even professionals sometimes have difficulty doing freehand. Beware of the word *Congratulations*. It's quite long and always seems to take up more room than you think!

Using a letterpress

Usually used on fondant or buttercream-frosted cakes where they can leave a mark, these ingenious gadgets allow you to build your message on a plaque, which you then press into the icing. An imprint is left behind for you to pipe over. There are various makes available, and they can be purchased from specialty stores or online suppliers (see Suppliers on page 165); alternatively, you can make your own.

1. Write your message in pencil on a piece of waxed paper. Turn the paper over so the message is backwards and place a small piece of clear acrylic on top. Place a No. 2 piping nozzle in a piping bag and pipe over the words with royal icing (Fig. a). Allow the lettering to dry.

2. Cover the cake with fondant or buttercream frosting. Turn the clear acrylic over and press into the cake to leave an imprint behind (Fig. b). Use this as a guide to pipe over.

Piped decorations

There are many types of piped royal icing decorations that you can make. Small models, such as the cradle on pages 128–9, are made in sections and then stuck together with royal icing. You can pipe onto fondant plaques, too. One of their main advantages is that they can be made well in advance. Store the finished decorations in a box away from dust and daylight.

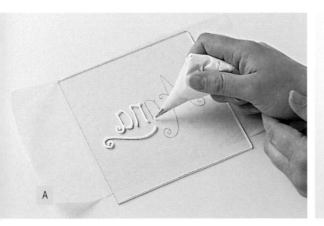

A

B

Run-outs

This technique of piping an outline, then flooding it with watered-down royal icing, is explained in full in the Baby's Cradle (see pages 128–9) and Snowflakes (see page 132–3) recipes.

However, as well as making shapes, run-outs can also be used to make lettering (Fig. c). When dry, gently ease the letters off the waxed paper with a palette knife and fix in place with a dab of royal icing.

Templates

Aside from the Wedding Star diagram, all of the templates on pages 120–1 are shown at 100%.

Baby's Cradle
(pages 128–9)

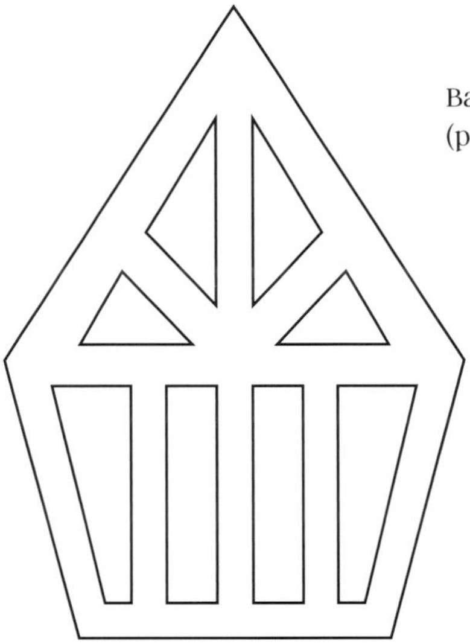

Canopy – make one of each

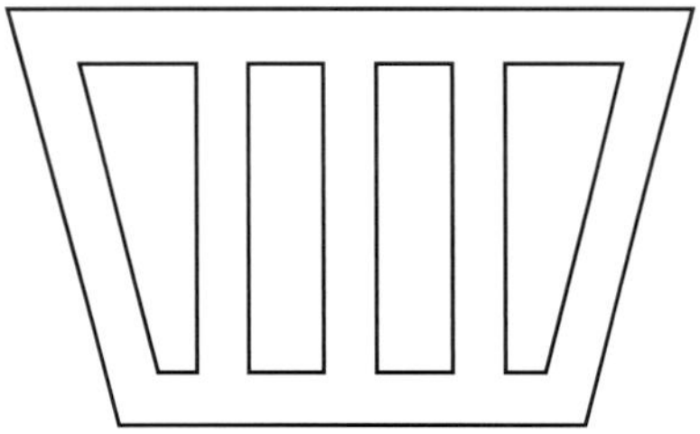

Headboard – make one

Rockers – make four

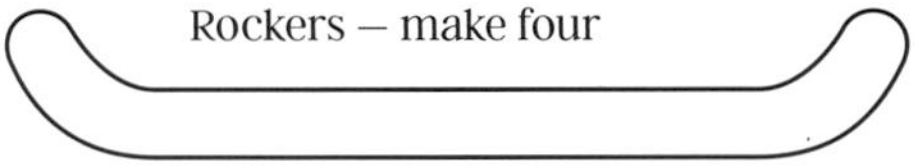

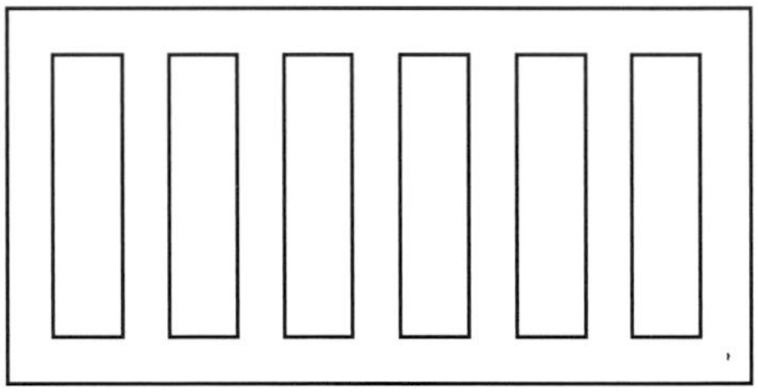

Foot – make one

Sides – make two

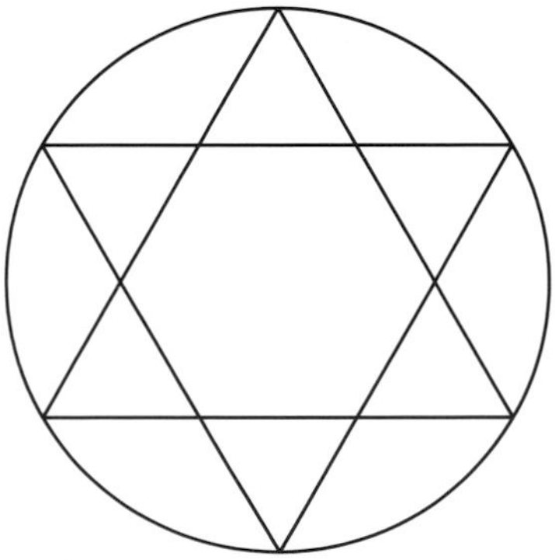

Wedding Star (pages 124–5)

Base – make one

Snowflakes (pages 132—3)

Christmas Bows

This simple idea makes a stunning Christmas centerpiece. It also works well with a more colorful ribbon selection.

INGREDIENTS
- 7 in. (18cm) round fruitcake (see pages 20–2)
- 3 Tbsp. brandy (optional)
- 3 Tbsp. boiled apricot jam
- Confectioners' sugar, for rolling out
- 1 lb. 5 oz. (650g) marzipan
- 1 quantity white royal icing (see page 106)

EQUIPMENT
- Carving knife
- Toothpick
- 9 in. (23cm) round cake board
- Pastry brush
- Rolling pin
- Cake smoother (optional)
- Spatula
- Small, sharp knife
- Palette knife
- 1 yd. (1m) silver and gold ribbon
- Scissors

TECHNIQUES
- Covering a fruitcake for fondant or swirled royal icing (see page 101)
- Creating peaked and swirled effects (see page 107)

1. Level the top of the cake and turn it upside down. Pierce the top a few times with a toothpick and drizzle brandy over the top.

2. Place on the cake board and brush the top and sides with boiled apricot jam.

3. Dust your work surface with confectioners' sugar and knead and roll out the marzipan. Lift the marzipan and place over the top of the cake. Smooth the top and sides, and trim around the base so it is neat.

4. Spread the royal icing over the cake and board. Swirl it into peaks using the palette knife (Fig. a). Leave the cake to dry.

5. When the icing has hardened, make four bows and stick them onto the cake with dabs of royal icing.

Variation

You can use any color scheme on this cake. Here, green and red ribbons give the cake a more vibrant and traditional look.

Tip Since this is a fruitcake, you can make and decorate the cake at the beginning of December to avoid a panic closer to Christmas.

Wedding Star

Stylish, elegant, modern—and best of all, easy to make. These instructions are based on using fruitcake and royal icing. However, you could use sponge cake as a base if you prefer. Just omit the marzipan and split, then fill and cover the cakes with scrumptious white chocolate ganache or buttercream frosting, instead of royal icing.

INGREDIENTS
- 1 lb. 2 oz. (500g) white fondant
- Confectioners' sugar, for rolling out
- 10 in. (25cm) round fruitcake
- 8 in. (20cm) round fruitcake (alternatively, you could use star-shaped baking pans)
- 5–6 Tbsp. brandy (optional)
- 4–5 Tbsp. boiled apricot jam
- 4½ lbs. (2.6kg) marzipan
- 2 quantities white royal icing (see page 106)

EQUIPMENT
- 13 in. (32cm) petal-shaped cake board or a 12 in. (30cm) round board
- 11 in. (28cm) petal-shaped cake board or a 10 in. (25cm) round board
- Rolling pin
- Cake smoother (optional)
- Small sharp knife
- Pencil
- Waxed or tracing paper
- Ruler
- Scissors
- Carving knife
- Pastry brush
- Palette knife
- Double-sided tape
- 3 yds. (3m) of ½ in. (1cm) white ribbon for edging boards (see page 34)
- Small square of aluminum foil
- 1 small candle
- About 20 rose leaves, washed and dried
- About 16 fresh-cut cream roses, washed, dried, and with stems cut off
- 2-tier cake stand (see page 35)

1. Cover the cake boards using the all-in-one method (see page 75). Use 8 oz. (250g) of the white fondant for the larger board and 5 oz. (150g) of the white fondant for the smaller one. Place to one side.

2. Make templates for the cakes. Trace around the pans used for baking the cakes. Draw two identical triangles inside each circle to create a star shape (see diagram on page 120). Cut out.

3. Place the relevant template on top of each cake and cut out (Fig. a).

4. Drizzle each cake with a little brandy if you wish and coat the top with boiled apricot jam.

5. Dust your work surface with confectioners' sugar and roll out 1 lb. 2 oz. (500g) of the marzipan. Run a knife underneath to check it's not stuck to the worktop and lay the largest cake upside down on the marzipan. Cut the marzipan around the cake then turn the cake the right way up.

6. Spread boiled apricot jam around the sides. Roll out 2 lb. 4 oz. (1kg) of the marzipan and cut out a strip about 38 in. (96cm) long and the same width as the height of the cake, including the marzipan topping.

7. Roll the strip into a loose bandage and unroll around the sides of the cake (Fig b). Because the icing will have a textured finish, it is not essential that all the sides be absolutely perfect; however it is important to make sure the cake is sealed in by the marzipan, and there are no holes anywhere.

8. Repeat the procedure on the smaller cake using about 12 oz. (350g) of marzipan for the top and 1½ oz. (750g) of marzipan for the sides.

9. Carefully place the cakes into position on the covered boards (see tip opposite). If the cake is well sealed, it can be left in this state in a cake box for up to two weeks, before icing.

10. When ready, cover the cakes with royal icing. Use a palette knife to apply the icing, swirling it into peaks as you go (see Fig. a on page 123). Leave a flattish area in the center of the smaller cake for the candle.

11. Stick some double-sided tape around the edges of the boards and then secure the ribbon in place. The ends of the ribbon should meet at the back of the cake.

12. Add the finishing touches to the cake on the day of the wedding. Place a candle on a small piece of aluminum foil in the center of the top cake. Lay one large rose leaf over a star point and place a rose on top. Continue around the candle and add a few extra leaves if you wish (Fig. c). Repeat on the lower cake and place the cakes on the stand.

Tip · · · · · · · · · · · · · · · ·

It is not advisable to use silk flowers with candles because of the possible risk of fire.

Although not essential, if you want to prevent the fondant beneath the cake from going soggy, place the relevant star template on top of the covered board and cut around it. Remove the icing from the center of the board, and when ready, set the marzipan-covered cake in the hole. Doing this will not affect the taste of the cake.

A

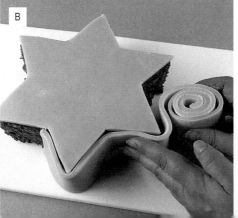

B

C

Christmas Stars

These stenciled stars are very easy to make and are incredibly effective. Depending on your chosen color scheme, you can leave them white or use silver or pale blue food coloring instead of gold. Instead of using traditional fruitcake covered with royal icing as a base, you could cover a marzipan-covered fruitcake or buttercream-frosted sponge cake with fondant instead.

Covering the cake

For fruitcake with marzipan and royal icing: Follow the instructions on pages 102 and 111. Use about 1 lb. 5 oz. (650g) of marzipan and two quantities of royal icing.

For fruitcake with marzipan and fondant: Follow the instructions on pages 101 and 74. Use about 1 lb. 5 oz. (650g) of marzipan and 1 lb. 2 oz. (500g) of the white fondant. Moisten the marzipan with water before covering it with the fondant.

For sponge cake with fondant: Split and fill the cake with buttercream frosting then spread frosting around the outside (see page 38). Follow the instructions on page 74 for covering with fondant. Use about 1 lb. 2 oz. (500g) of the white fondant.

INGREDIENTS

- See "Covering the cake," right, for the amount of icing required to cover the cake
- 7 in. (18cm) round sponge cake or fruitcake (see pages 13–4 and 20–2)
- 1 quantity white royal icing (see page 106), for making stars
- 3 Tbsp. brandy (optional)
- 3 Tbsp. boiled apricot jam
- Confectioners' sugar, for rolling out
- 1 lb. 5 oz. (650g) marzipan
- Edible gold food coloring
- Edible gold and/or silver balls

EQUIPMENT

- Pencil
- Waxed paper or parchment paper
- Scalpel
- Ruler
- 9 in. (23cm) round cake board
- Palette knife
- Paintbrush

TECHNIQUES

- Filling the cake (see page 38)
- Covering with buttercream (see page 38)
- Covering a fruitcake for fondant or swirled royal icing (see page 101)
- Covering a round fruitcake for smooth royal icing (see page 102)
- Royal-icing a round fruitcake (see page 111)

1. Trace the star shapes onto the paper and cut them out using the scalpel and ruler. Make at least eight since you may only be able to use them once.

2. If not already in place, put the covered cake on the cake board. Place the stencil on the cake and stipple some royal icing onto the cake's surface using the flat edge of a palette knife (Fig. a).

3. Lift the stencil off the cake's surface and repeat the process over the sides and top.

4. When you have finished the stars, spread a covering of royal icing over the exposed cake board. Use the flat side of the knife to pat the icing to form little peaks. Allow the cake to dry.

5. When the royal icing has set, pick out the stencil with the gold food coloring. Hold the brush almost flat and stroke it across the stars so that the food coloring coats the tips of the icing peaks (Fig. b). Do the same on the cake board.

6. Stick edible gold balls over the cake to fill the spaces between the stars.

Tips

If you don't want to make your own stencils, you may be able to find washable, reusable, plastic star-shaped stencils at specialty stores or online suppliers (see Suppliers on page 165).

You may find it helpful to use tweezers to handle the gold balls since they are tiny.

A

B

Baby's Cradle

This pretty little cradle is made using a technique called royal icing run-outs. The outline of each crib section is piped with royal icing and then flooded with slightly watered-down icing. It may take a little bit of practice to get this technique right, but the results are worthwhile. One advantage to run-outs is that they can be made up to a month in advance. Prepare and ice the cake in exactly the same way as the Christening Cake on pages 98–9. Use blue or pink as appropriate.

INGREDIENTS
(For the cradle only)
- 1 quantity white royal icing (see page 106)
- ½ oz. (15g) white fondant
- ⅛ oz. (5g) flesh-colored fondant
- Food color for baby's hair
- ½ oz. (15g) blue fondant

EQUIPMENT
(For the cradle only)
- Pencil
- Tracing paper
- Waxed or parchment paper
- Board or tray
- Masking tape
- Small cups or bowls
- Palette knife
- Piping bags (see page 113)
- No. 1 piping nozzle
- Scissors
- Small soft paintbrush
- Drinking straw
- Tiny ribbon bow

TECHNIQUES
- Run-outs (see page 119)
- Modeling with fondant (see page 82)

1. Trace the templates of the cradle components (see page 120) onto tracing paper.

2. Place a piece of waxed or parchment paper onto something flat, such as a board or tray, and hold it in place with a small piece of tape at each corner. Slide the tracing paper with the template underneath the waxed or parchment paper. Leave an end poking out so you can move it around freely beneath the top paper.

3. Place about 1 Tbsp. of white royal icing into a cup and beat it thoroughly with a knife to expel any air. Stir in a couple drops of water to help it flow through the tiny piping nozzle more easily.

4. Place the icing into a piping bag fitted with a No. 1 piping nozzle. Close the bag and pipe the outlines of the cradle components.

5. Pipe at least two sides, one pointed end, one bottom end, two canopies, four rockers, and one base. It would be wise to pipe extras of each shape as the run-outs will be fragile.

6. To make the icing for flooding, place two heaping tablespoons of royal icing into a bowl. Add water drop by drop. Mix until the consistency is such that when you lift the knife out, the tail it leaves disappears on a count of three.

7. Tip or spoon the icing into a piping bag. Close the bag and snip a tiny triangle off the end. Gently squeeze the bag, and using a gentle wiggling motion, fill one of the shapes. Use the tip of a soft, damp paintbrush to coax it into any obstinate corners (Fig. a). Allow it to dry for at least 24 hours.

8. When dry, peel the backing off the shapes. Turn the canopy sections over and pipe crisscrossing lines on the back (Fig. b). Stick two sets of rockers together and let these and the canopies dry.

9. To make the pillow, make a tiny, white fondant rectangle. Using the tip of a paintbrush handle, press a line of indents down each shorter side to look like a frill (Fig. c).

10. Make a flesh-colored ball for the head. Use a paintbrush handle to gently push a small dent into the side of the head to resemble a forehead. Make a tiny "U" impression using the end of a drinking straw, so it looks like a closed eye.

11. Stick the head on the pillow and place both on the cradle base. Add a small fondant oval for the body. Add a tiny flesh ball for his ear and press a small hollow into it with the brush handle. Paint hair with food coloring.

12. Carefully stick the sides and the two ends of the cradle around the base using royal icing.

13. Make a tiny white fondant rectangle for the sheet and a larger blue one for the blanket.

14. Using the back of the knife, press a crisscross pattern into the blanket and lay it on the edge of the white sheet, leaving about half the white still protruding. Fold the white back over the blue and lay the blanket over the baby.

15. Stick the canopy sections in place. Stick the rockers onto the base of the crib. (You could place a small ball of fondant underneath the cradle to add support while the rockers are drying.)

16. Roll two white fondant balls and stick on the two ends of the crib. Stick a tiny bow on top of the canopy. Let it dry for 24 hours.

𝒯ip · · · · · · · · · · · · · · · · ·

Use a soft, damp paintbrush to smooth away any unwanted blobs of icing along the joins of the cradle.

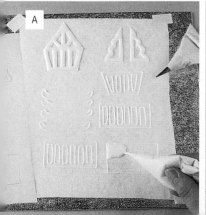

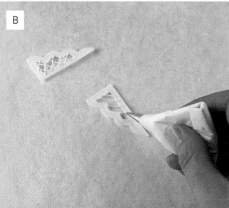

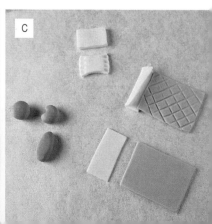

Piped Flowers

A spiral of pretty piped flowers winds its way around the cake. You could make the flowers up to a month in advance. You can cover the cake with fondant and use sponge cake instead of a fruitcake if you prefer.

INGREDIENTS
- See "Covering the cake," right, for the amount of icing required to cover cake
- 6 in. (15cm) round sponge cake or fruitcake (see pages 13–4 and 20–2)
- 1 quantity royal icing (see page 106)
- Pink, purple, green, and yellow paste food coloring

EQUIPMENT
- 8 in. (20cm) round cake board
- Scissors
- Waxed paper or parchment paper
- No. 57, No. 58, or No. 59 petal piping nozzles
- Piping bags (see page 113)
- Small bowls for mixing food coloring
- Icing nail (or a cork stuck onto a long nail)
- No. 2 piping nozzle
- Fine paintbrush
- Leaf nozzle

TECHNIQUES
- Covering a fruitcake for fondant or swirled royal icing (see page 101)
- Covering a round fruitcake for smooth royal icing (see page 102)
- Covering a cake with fondant (see page 74)
- Royal-icing a round fruitcake (see page 111)
- Piping flowers (see page 117)
- Creating different piping effects (see pages 115–6)

Covering the cake

For fruitcake with marzipan and royal icing: Follow the instructions on pages 102 and 111. Use about 1 lb. 4 oz. (600g) of marzipan and two quantities of royal icing. When the cake has hardened, cover the cake board with royal icing as well (see page 112).

For fruitcake with marzipan and fondant: Follow the instructions on pages 101 and 74. Use about 1 lb. 4 oz. (600g) of marzipan and 1 lb. 2 oz. (500g) of white fondant. Moisten the marzipan with water before covering it with the fondant. Cover the cake board using the bandage method shown on page 75.

For sponge cake with fondant: Split and fill the cake with buttercream frosting then spread the frosting around the outside. Roll out 1 lb. 2 oz. (500g) of white fondant and cover the cake. Cover the cake board using the bandage method shown on page 75.

1. Cut out at least 40 waxed paper squares. Place a petal nozzle into a piping bag. Add 2 Tbsp. of pink or purple icing. Fold over the end of the bag to close it.

2. Stick a paper square on the top of the piping nail with a dab of icing. With the thick end of the piping nozzle in the center of the flower, squeeze the bag and turn the nail. Slightly lift the thin edge of the nozzle as you turn to form a petal. Release the pressure and pull away.

3. Wipe the end of the nozzle. Tuck the nozzle just underneath the edge of the first petal and pipe a second. Repeat making five petals (Fig. a). This is tricky, so you will need practice.

4. Make about 20 pink and 20 purple flowers and let them dry on the waxed paper backings for at least 24 hours.

5. When the flowers are ready, place about 2 tablespoons of white royal icing into a piping bag fitted with a No. 2 piping nozzle. Pipe a "snail trail" around the base of the cake.

Squeeze a little icing out of the bag, release the pressure and pull slightly to the side, so that the icing tapers and falls onto the cake. Continue like this until you have piped around the whole base.

6. Using a little watered-down food color, paint a spiral guideline around the cake. Start at the base of the cake and work around it. Try to keep the width between the lines fairly equal (Fig. b).

7. Peel the backing paper off the flowers and stick the flowers on the cake with dabs of royal icing.

8. Place about 1 Tbsp. of yellow royal icing in a piping bag with a No. 2 piping nozzle. Pipe a dot in the center of each flower.

9. Place a leaf nozzle in a piping bag and add 2 Tbsp. of green royal icing. Pipe leaves between the flowers. Squeeze the icing out, release the pressure and pull to create a leaf shape.

Tips · · · · · · · ·

You could make the summer flowers on pages 60–1 from royal icing and use these to decorate the cake instead.

An easier, but still effective alternative to using piped flowers would be to use fondant plunge cutter blossoms (see page 81).

A

B

Snowflakes

These snowflakes are made using the royal icing run-out technique that is also used on the Baby's Cradle on pages 128-9. If you don't wish to do all the piping, you could cut snowflake shapes out of edible decorating paper. If you prefer, you can use a sponge cake instead of a fruitcake and cover it with fondant instead of royal icing.

INGREDIENTS
- See "Covering the cake," right, for the amount of icing required to cover the cake
- 8 in. (20cm) round sponge cake or fruitcake (see pages 13–4 and 20–2)
- 2 quantities white royal icing (for snowflakes; see page 106)
- Blue paste food coloring

EQUIPMENT
- 10 in. (25cm) round cake board
- Pencil
- Tracing paper
- Waxed or parchment paper
- Board or tray
- Masking tape
- Small cups or bowls
- Palette knife
- Piping bags (see page 113)
- No. 1 piping nozzle
- Scissors
- Paintbrush
- No.2 Piping nozzle

TECHNIQUES
- Covering a fruitcake for fondant or swirled royal icing (see page 101)
- Covering a round fruitcake for smooth royal icing (see page 102)
- Covering a cake with fondant (see page 74)
- Royal-icing a round fruitcake (see page 111)
- Run-outs (see page 119)
- Creating different piping effects (see pages 115–6)

Covering the cake

For fruitcake with marzipan and royal icing: See pages 102 and 111. Use about 1 lb. 10 oz. (800g) of marzipan and two quantities royal icing. Stir a little blue food coloring into the royal icing before coating the cake and cake board.

For fruitcake with marzipan and fondant: Follow the instructions on pages 101 and 74. Use about 1 lb. 10 oz. (800g) of marzipan and 1 lb. 10 oz. (800g) of the pale blue fondant. Moisten the marzipan with water before covering it with the fondant. Cover the exposed cake board using the leftover fondant and the bandage technique shown on page 75.

For sponge cake with fondant: Split and fill the cake with buttercream frosting then spread the frosting around the outside. Roll out and cover the cake with 1 lb. 10 oz. (800g) of pale blue fondant. Cover the exposed cake board with the leftover fondant using the bandage technique shown on page 75.

1. Trace the snowflake templates on page 121 onto tracing paper. Place a piece of waxed or parchment paper onto something flat such as a board or tray and hold it in place with a piece of tape at each corner. Slide the tracing paper with the template underneath the waxed or parchment paper (see Fig. a on page 129).

2. Place about 1 Tbsp. of white royal icing into a small cup or bowl and beat it thoroughly with a knife to expel any air. Stir in a couple drops of water to help it flow through the tiny piping nozzle more easily. The icing should still hold its shape when piped.

3. Place the icing into a piping bag fitted with a No. 1 piping nozzle. Pipe over the outlines of the snowflakes. Pipe at least 16 outlines to allow for breakages (see Fig. a on page 129).

4. Place about 2 Tbsp. of royal icing into a bowl. Add a few drops of water and mix in. Continue to add water, drop by drop, and mix it in until the icing has reached such a consistency that when you lift the knife out, the tail it leaves behind disappears on a count of three.

5. Tip or spoon the icing into a piping bag. Close the bag and snip a tiny triangle off the end. Gently squeeze the end and, using a gentle wiggling motion, fill one of the shapes (see Fig. a on page 129). Use the tip of a soft, damp paintbrush to coax it into any obstinate corners. Allow the shapes to dry for at least 24 hours.

6. Place about 1 Tbsp. of royal icing into a piping bag fitted with a No. 2 piping nozzle. Pipe a "snail trail" around the base of the cake. Squeeze out a bit of icing, release the pressure, and pull slightly to the side so that the icing forms a tail. Repeat all the way around the cake (Fig. a).

7. When the snowflakes are dry, slide a palette knife beneath them to gently ease them off the paper (Fig. b).

8. Place the snowflakes into position and stick with dabs of royal icing.

9. Pipe royal icing dots between the snowflakes to finish off (Fig. c).

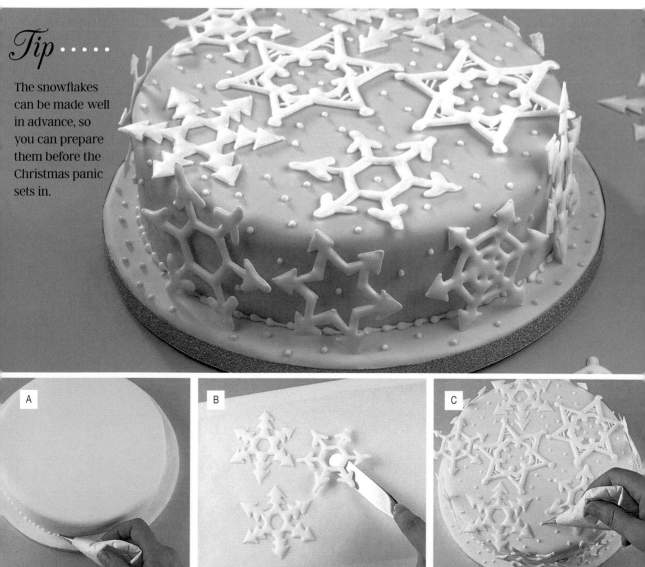

Tip · · · · ·

The snowflakes can be made well in advance, so you can prepare them before the Christmas panic sets in.

A

B

C

CHOCOLATE

As well as being delicious, chocolate is extremely versatile, too. It can be used to cover a cake, molded into decorations, or mixed with cream to make ganache. This chapter contains ideas for all sorts of occasions. There's even a simple recipe for truffles that uses up all those leftover pieces of cake (see page 141).

Types of chocolate

There are four basic grades of chocolate to choose from, and all are available in dark, milk, or white forms. I would advise that you use either dessert or baking chocolate since they are easy to handle.

Dessert or eating chocolate: Dark chocolate has the strongest flavor and tends to be quite hard when you bite into it. Milk chocolate is softer to the bite and sweeter. White is sweeter still and actually doesn't taste of chocolate at all. All of these types can be used in cooking. A purist would argue that you should only use dark chocolate containing a minimum of 70 percent cocoa solids for cooking, but the choice is yours.

Couverture: Because it is made entirely with cocoa butter, couverture is the most expensive type of chocolate and is considered by most experts to be the best chocolate to use in cooking. However, it has to be tempered (heated and cooled to an exact temperature) before use so it's not that easy for a beginner to use.

Baking/cooking chocolate: This type of chocolate melts easily and is ideal for the beginner. The taste varies from brand to brand and, in fact, some supermarket brands are now so good it is very hard to tell them apart from dessert chocolate.

Chocolate-flavored cake covering: This is not actually chocolate at all; it is merely chocolate flavored. The taste is weak, and it tends to have a soft, greasy texture. It melts and sets very quickly, which can be useful if you are in a hurry. Because it is much cheaper than any other type of chocolate, it may be worth using it to experiment with your technique, particularly if you have never worked with chocolate before.

You can make all sorts of decorations using chocolate, all of which are very easy to make. These include chocolate leaves, run-outs, squiggles, and shapes. (See pages 139–40 for instructions.)

A

Melting chocolate

When melting chocolate, you must not get any
water, steam, or condensation in the chocolate. If
you do, it will become thick, gritty, and unusable.
You can use a double boiler or follow the
instructions below.

1. Break the chocolate into small pieces and place
    in a heatproof bowl (Fig. a).

2. Place the bowl over a saucepan of water. The
    water should not touch the base of the bowl.
    Heat the water and simmer until the chocolate
    has melted (Fig. b).

Alternative method

Break the chocolate into pieces into a bowl that
is microwave-safe. Heat on high for 90 seconds.
Stir and repeat. Don't let the chocolate overcook;
otherwise, it will burn.

B

Covering a cake with melted chocolate

A simple way to cover a cake is to pour chocolate over it. The cake can be plain or pre-iced with ganache.

1. Place the cake on a rack and pour the chocolate over the top (Fig. a). The cake must be at room temperature.

2. Lightly bang the rack up and down a few times to encourage the chocolate to fully cover the cake and to dislodge any air bubbles (Fig. b). Allow the chocolate to set.

A

B

Chocolate ganache

Ganache is a spread made out of a mixture of cream and melted chocolate. Made using white or dark chocolate, it can be used to fill and cover gateau-type cakes, but would not usually be used with fondant designs.

INGREDIENTS
- 10 oz. (300g) dark or white chocolate, broken into pieces
- 2½ cups (600ml) heavy cream

1. Place the broken chocolate into a large bowl.

2. Gently heat the cream in a saucepan and bring up to boiling point. Remove from the heat and pour over the chocolate.

3. Let sit for 3 minutes then stir until the chocolate has melted.

4. Allow the chocolate to cool completely, then whisk to a light, whipped consistency. Cover and place in the refrigerator for at least 30 minutes or until needed.

5. When ready to use, remove from the refrigerator. If the chocolate mixture is still a little sloppy, beat until thick.

c

Piping with ganache

It is also possible to pipe with chocolate ganache. You can pipe a milk chocolate border onto a cake that has been covered in white chocolate, or vice versa (Fig. c). Add some chocolate leaves or a few chocolate-dipped fruit for a stylish yet simple cake for a special occasion.

Chocolate leaves

An effective decoration, chocolate leaves are incredibly easy to make.

1. Select some well-proportioned rose leaves. Wash and dry them on paper towels.

2. Melt some chocolate (see page 136). Hold a leaf by the stalk and press the underside (this side produces a better vein effect) into the melted chocolate. Allow them to dry on waxed paper.

3. When the leaves have set, carefully peel the real leaf off the chocolate one (see Fig. b on page 161).

Dipped fruit

You can use semisweet, milk, or white chocolate and many different kinds of fruit, including strawberries, grapes, and cherries.

1. Wash and dry the fruit on paper towels. Melt the chocolate (see page 136).

2. Dip the fruit into the chocolate so that it is half-covered. Allow them to set on waxed paper (Fig. d).

D

Chocolate run-outs

Another way to make simple shapes is to make run-outs. The basic principle is exactly the same as for making royal icing run-outs (see page 119). You can vary the colors, too—pipe an outline with dark chocolate and fill it with white, for example.

1. Place some melted chocolate into a piping bag. Fold the end of the bag to close it and snip a triangle off the end.

2. Pipe the outline of a simple shape, such as a heart, onto waxed paper or parchment paper.

3. Place some more melted chocolate in another bag. Snip a bigger triangle off the end and fill in the chocolate outline (Fig. e).

E

Chocolate shapes

There are several ways of making decorative chocolate shapes and both are very simple.

Solid shapes

Cut the shapes you want out of edible decorating paper. Dip one side of the paper shape into melted chocolate. Allow it to dry. Since it is edible, you can either leave the paper on or peel it off. This technique is used and explained in full in the Chocolate Shapes (see pages 154–5) and Chocolate Extravaganza (see pages 158–9) recipes.

Squiggles or shape outlines

Simply pipe the shape using melted chocolate onto a sheet of waxed paper and then let set.

Chocolate modeling paste

There are all sorts of different ways to make chocolate modeling paste, but the easiest way is to knead some cocoa powder into a piece of marzipan. There are no hard and fast rules about amounts; obviously, the more cocoa powder you add, the darker the color will be. Use as normal marzipan (see page 104).

If the marzipan is hard to knead, microwave it for 10 to 15 seconds to soften it. Repeat if necessary but don't overdo it, otherwise the oils in the marzipan could get very hot and burn.

Quick chocolate rose

This is a very simple way to make a rose using chocolate modeling paste. Of course, it would work using uncolored marzipan and fondant, too (Fig. a).

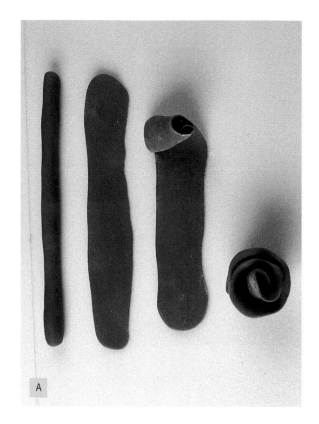

A

1. Take about ½ oz. (15g) of chocolate marzipan. Roll it into a thin sausage shape.

2. Flatten the sausage shape into a thin strip. Press along one long edge to make it thinner. Paint a line of water along the other long edge.

3. Carefully roll the marzipan up like a bandage; the thinnest edge should form the flower.

4. Tweak the edges slightly to improve the rose shape.

B

Chocolate truffles

This is a great way to use up those leftover pieces of cake. This recipe works equally well using sponge cake, chocolate cake, or fruitcake and any type of chocolate.

1. Break up the cake into crumbs and place in a bowl.

2. Melt some chocolate. You will need approximately 1 oz. (30g) of chocolate for every 1 oz (30 g) of cake crumb.

C

3. Stir the chocolate into the crumbs (Fig. b).

4. Roll the mixture into balls. Place in petit fours cases if you wish.

5. Decorate with melted chocolate and candies (fig. c).

Templates

All of the templates on pages 140−3 are shown at 100%.

Cocoa Painting
(pages 150−1)

Make five

Patterns for plaques

Marzipan Chocolates (pages 146-7)

Chocolate Shapes (pages 154—5);
make nine of each shape

Quick Chocolate Cake

This cake has been decorated using simple techniques. It's a traditional cake that's great for any occasion—it looks just perfect, yet is so easy to make.

INGREDIENTS
- Two 7 in. (18cm) chocolate cakes baked in layer cake pans
- 1 quantity buttercream frosting (see page 37)
- 1 tsp. cocoa powder
- Decoration for top of cake (lattice shapes, leaves, candies, and so on; see Suppliers on page 165)

EQUIPMENT
- Palette knife
- 8 in. (20cm) round cake board or plate
- Paper doily
- Small sifter or tea strainer

TECHNIQUES
- Chocolate cake (see page 16)
- Filling the cake (see page 38)
- Covering with buttercream (see page 38)

1. Sandwich the two cake layers together with a liberal spreading of buttercream frosting. Place the cake on the cake board. Spread the frosting smoothly over the top of the cake.

2. Lay the paper doily on top of the cake. Place the cocoa powder in the sifter and gently tap it, moving it over the doily (Fig. a).

3. Carefully lift the doily to reveal a pattern underneath (Fig. b).

4. Place a dab of frosting and a few chocolate decorations in the center of the cake to finish off.

Tips

Chocolate leaves are easy to make if you want to keep the whole design homemade. See page 138 to find out how to make them.

You can freeze the frosted cake if you wish. Allow it to defrost thoroughly and make sure that all of the condensation has evaporated before decorating it with the cocoa.

Instead of using cocoa, you could decorate the cake with candies or chocolate buttons instead.

Marzipan Chocolates

This is a very easy cake to put together. The difficult part is stopping yourself from nibbling and sampling as you go!

INGREDIENTS
- Confectioners' sugar, for rolling out
- 8 oz. (250g) golden marzipan
- 5 oz. (150g) milk chocolate
- 6 in. (15cm) round sponge cake (see page 13)
- 2 quantities chocolate buttercream frosting (see page 37) or 1 quantity chocolate ganache (see page 137)

EQUIPMENT
- Rolling pin
- Assorted cutters or templates (see page 143)
- Heatproof bowl
- Small saucepan
- Cooling rack
- Carving knife
- Palette knife
- 8 in. (20cm) round cake board

TECHNIQUES
- Melting chocolate (see page 136)
- Filling the cake (see page 38)
- Covering with buttercream (see page 38)
- Chocolate ganache (see page 137)

1. Prepare the chocolates. Dust your work surface with confectioners' sugar and knead and roll out the marzipan to a thickness of about ¼ in. (5mm). Using the cutters, cut out about 40 shapes (Fig. a), or use the templates on page 143.

2. Melt the milk chocolate in a heatproof bowl. Dip each shape into the chocolate and place on a cooling rack to harden (Fig. b).

3. When the chocolates are set, prepare the cake. Slice the cake into two or three layers and then sandwich back together with buttercream frosting or ganache. Place the cake on a cake board.

4. Spread and swirl the frosting over the outside of the cake. Press the marzipan shapes into the chocolate covering.

Variation

Put a few marzipan chocolates into a box to create a lovely little hostess gift or a surprise for a friend.

Easter Cake

Here's a cake that's simple to put together and one that will brighten any Easter table.

INGREDIENTS
- 1¾ oz. (50g) milk chocolate
- 1¾ oz. (50g) shredded wheat cereal
- 6 in. (15cm) round sponge cake (see page 13)
- 1 quantity chocolate buttercream frosting (see page 37)
- Mini chocolate eggs

EQUIPMENT
- Heatproof bowl
- Small saucepan
- Small bowl to use as mold, for nest
- Carving knife
- Palette knife
- 8 in. (20cm) round cake board
- About 6 chicks for decoration

TECHNIQUES
- Melting chocolate (see page 136)
- Filling the cake (see page 38)
- Covering with buttercream (see page 38)

1. To make the nest, melt the chocolate and break up the cereal. Mix the two together and spoon the mixture into a small bowl (Fig. a). Let set.

2. To prepare the cake, level the top and turn the cake upside down. Split it into two or three layers and reassemble, filling the layers with buttercream frosting.

3. Place the cake on the cake board and cover the top, sides and exposed cake board with frosting.

4. Press a line of chocolate eggs around the top and bottom of the cake (Fig. b).

5. When the nest has set, place it on top of the cake and fill it with little chicks. Add a few extra eggs as well if you wish.

Variation

This cake (below left) was decorated with an Easter teddy bear whose body is a chocolate egg.

To make him, roll 1 oz. (30g) golden marzipan into a sausage for his legs. Place the egg in the center and bend the marzipan around it to hold the egg steady. Shape the ends into feet.

Make a ½ oz. (15g) marzipan ball for his head and stick it on top of the egg. Add a marzipan oval for his nose and two tiny balls for his ears. Press the end of a paintbrush into each ear and into the lower part of his nose to make a mouth. Add three black dots of food coloring for his eyes and nose.

Make two ⅛ oz. (5g) sausage shapes for his arms and stick onto the body.

To avoid arguments, you may want to make enough spare teddy bears so everyone can have one!

Tips ····

Instead of using store-bought chocolate eggs, you could make your own eggs out of fondant or you could use sugared almonds.

A

B

Cocoa Painting

Cocoa painting, which is a traditional but often overlooked technique, is used to create special effects on a cake. Using this technique, you can paint a pattern on a cake, or you can paint an actual photo, perhaps of a much-loved pet or a favorite place. The cocoa gives the image a sepia look, resembling that of an old photograph. You can do a cocoa painting directly on a cake or, as in this painting, on plaques.

INGREDIENTS
- 10 oz. (300g) white fondant
- Confectioners' sugar, for rolling out
- 1 tsp. vegetable shortening
- 1 tsp. cocoa powder
- 6 in. (15cm) square sponge cake (see page 13)
- 2 quantities chocolate buttercream frosting (see page 37)

EQUIPMENT
- Rolling pin
- Cutter or template (see page 142), for plaques
- Saucer
- Small saucepan
- Fine paintbrush
- Scalpel
- Carving knife
- Palette knife
- 8 in. (20cm) square cake board
- Star piping nozzle (optional; see tip opposite)
- Piping bag (see page 113)

TECHNIQUES
- Plaques (see page 82)
- Filling the cake (see page 38)
- Covering with buttercream (see page 38)
- Creating different piping effects (see pages 115–6)

1. To make the plaques, roll out the fondant and cut out a thin oval, either with a cutter or using the template on page 142. Cut out four more, kneading and re-rolling the fondant as necessary. If you have time, let them harden for 12 hours, turning each over after 5 to 6 hours.

2. To paint the plaques, melt a little vegetable shortening on a saucer over a pan of hot water. Remove the pan from the heat but leave the saucer in place while you work so the shortening will stay melted.

3. Mix a little cocoa powder and melted shortening together with the paintbrush (Fig. a).

4. Lightly paint the outline of the picture on a plaque and fill it in (Fig. b). If you do not want to paint the pattern freehand, trace the patterns on page 142 and scribe them onto the plaque (see page 82). Remember that you can always add more but you can't take it off, so build the picture up gradually.

5. If you want to create highlights or thin line effects, you can scratch little pieces off with the tip of a clean, sharp scalpel (Fig. c).

6. Level the top of the cake and turn it upside down. Slice into two or three layers and reassemble it, filling the layers with buttercream frosting.

7. Place the cake on the cake board and spread frosting over the top and sides. Spread frosting over the exposed areas of the cake board as well.

8. Place the plaques into position. Press them gently into the frosting to hold them in place.

9. Place a star piping nozzle into a piping bag and spoon 2 to 3 Tbsp. of frosting into the bag. Pipe around the outsides of the plaques and the edges and base of the cake. Vary the shades of brown if you wish by adding more cocoa to the frosting.

Tips If you don't want to pipe frosting onto the cake, stick chocolate buttons or other chocolate candies around it instead.

If you wish to use candles, stand them in the chocolate frosting on top of the cake. Don't try to poke them through the fondant plaque.

A

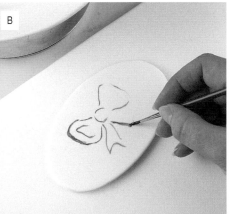

B

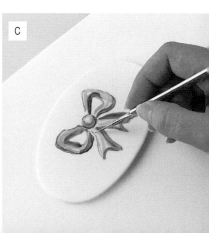

C

Chocolate Feathers

You can make the chocolate feathers a few days in advance if you wish. Just store them in a dry place, where people won't be tempted to steal them!

INGREDIENTS
- 4 oz. (100g) milk chocolate
- 4 oz. (100g) dark chocolate
- 4 oz. (100g) white chocolate
- 8 in. (20cm) round sponge cake (see page 13)
- 2 quantities white chocolate buttercream frosting (see page 37) or 1 quantity white chocolate ganache (see page 137)

EQUIPMENT
- Waxed or parchment paper
- Tray
- Heatproof bowls, for melting chocolate
- Small saucepan
- Piping bags (see page 113)
- Cup
- Scissors
- Sharp pointed knife
- Carving knife
- Palette knife
- 10 in. (25cm) round cake board

TECHNIQUES
- Melting chocolate (see page 136)
- Making a piping bag (see page 114)
- Filling the cake (see page 38)
- Covering with buttercream (see page 38)

1. Make the feathers first so they have time to harden. Place a large sheet of waxed paper on a tray. Melt the milk chocolate in a bowl, either in a microwave or over a pan of simmering water.

2. Place a piping bag into a cup and tip in some of the chocolate. Carefully fold over the ends of the bag to close it and snip a tiny triangle off the end.

3. Pipe a thick line (it can be either straight or wavy) of chocolate onto the waxed or parchment paper (Fig. a). It's not essential to use a bag; you can drizzle a line with a spoon if you prefer, but a bag makes things much easier and less sticky.

4. Using the tip of a sharp knife, poke and drag the chocolate from the center of the line outwards to make a point. Continue down both sides of the line, fanning the chocolate outward (Fig. b). Make about 20 to allow for breakages and chocolate thieves!

5. Repeat this procedure with the dark and white chocolate and let harden in a cool, dry place.

6. When the feathers are ready, prepare the cake. Level the top and turn it upside down. Slice it into two or three horizontal layers and reassemble it, sandwiching the layers together with buttercream frosting.

7. Put the cake on the cake board. Spread the frosting around the sides and top of the cake.

8. Gently slide a palette knife under a feather and ease it off the backing paper. Place the feather in position on the cake. Make a ring around the base and top of the cake and place a few in the center.

• •

Tips   Make the piped lines of chocolate quite thick. If the feathers are too thin, they will snap and be impossible to use. You can also mix colors by piping a line of milk and white chocolate together.

If you plan to use candles, use white ones and place them inside the top ring of feathers, away from the central feathers.

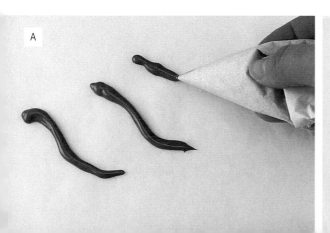

A

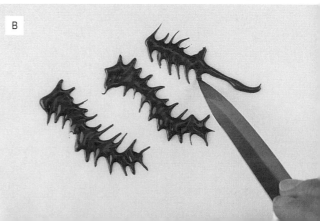

B

Chocolate Shapes

Dipping edible decorative paper into melted chocolate is an easy way to make various chocolate shapes. Because the paper is edible, you can either leave it on the back or peel it off after the shapes have hardened.

INGREDIENTS

- 3½ oz. (100g) milk chocolate
- 3½ oz. (100g) dark chocolate
- 6 in. (15cm) round sponge cake (see page 13)
- 2 quantities white chocolate buttercream frosting (see page 37) or 1 quantity white chocolate ganache (see page 137)

EQUIPMENT

- Edible decorating paper
- Pencil
- Scissors
- Waxed or parchment paper
- Tray
- Heatproof bowl
- Small saucepan
- Piping bags (see page 113)
- 8 in. (20cm) round cake board
- Carving knife
- Palette knife

TECHNIQUES

- Melting chocolate (see page 136)
- Filling the cake (see page 38)
- Covering with buttercream (see page 38)

1. Using edible decorating paper, trace and cut out about nine each of the heart, square, circle, moon, and star templates (see page 143). Cut just inside the pencil marks.

2. Place some waxed or parchment paper on a tray.

3. Melt the milk chocolate. Dip a paper shape into the chocolate (Fig. a). Coat one side, then place onto the tray.

4. Make four or five shapes. Holding both edges of the tray, bang it on your work surface a couple of times to dislodge any air bubbles.

5. Repeat this procedure until half of the paper shapes have been used.

6. Tip any leftover melted chocolate into a piping bag. Fold the end to close it and snip a tiny triangle off the end. Pipe a squiggle directly onto the covered tray (Fig. b).

7. Repeat the above procedure with the dark chocolate.

8. When the chocolate shapes have set, prepare the cake. Slice it into three layers and reassemble, filling the layers with the buttercream frosting or ganache.

9. Put the cake on the cake board. Spread a thick coating of frosting or ganache around the outside of the cake.

10. Peel the paper off the shapes (or you can leave it on since it's edible) and press them into the frosting.

Tips
If you're feeling really ambitious, you can pipe the recipient's name in chocolate, either in single letters or cursive writing.

If you are using candles, keep them lit them for as little time as possible since the heat might melt the chocolate.

Monster Cupcake

This cake is baked in an oven-safe glass bowl to give it its authentic shape. The enormous paper cupcake liner is actually a precut paper liner that you can purchase from specialty stores or online suppliers (see Suppliers on page 165).

INGREDIENTS
- 1 chocolate glass bowl cake (see pages 13 and 14 and step 1, right)
- Confectioners' sugar, for rolling out
- 5 oz. (150g) white fondant
- ½ oz. (15g) red fondant
- 2¾ oz. (75g) gray fondant
- Black food coloring or black food-coloring pen

EQUIPMENT
- 6 in. (15cm) round precut paper liners for cakes
- Rolling pin
- Sharp knife
- Paintbrush
- About 7 in. (18cm) round plate or cake board

TECHNIQUES
- Baking a glass bowl cake (see page 14)
- Fondant (see page 72)

1. Mix up a three-egg sponge cake mixture (see page 13). Add 1 Tbsp. of cocoa. Place the liner in the bowl, add the mixture, and bake.

2. When the cake is cool, roll out the white fondant. Holding a sharp knife virtually upright cut out a wiggly, vaguely circular shape for the white topping (Fig. a). Set aside the excess.

3. Place the topping on the cake. Roll about ⅓ oz. (10g) of red fondant into a ball for the cherry and stick on top of the cake with a dab of water.

4. To make the mouse, roll about 1½ oz. (50g) of gray fondant into a conical shape for the mouse's body. Bend the pointed end over to form the head (Fig. b). Using the end of a paintbrush, poke an oval hole for his outraged mouth.

5. Make two ⅛ oz. (5g) oval shapes for the feet and stick onto either side of his body. Make a couple of tiny lines in the end of each foot with the tip of the knife.

6. Make two tiny white balls for the eyes and stick onto the head with little dabs of water. Add tiny black dots for the pupils using black food coloring and a fine brush or a black food-coloring pen.

7. Knead a tiny bit of red fondant into a little bit of white to make a pink color. Make a tiny ball for the nose and a wiggly string for the tail. Stick both in position and press a few lines down the length of the tail.

8. Make two tiny gray strings for arms. Bend into "S" shapes and stick onto the side of the body. Make two tiny gray ball shapes for the ears and stick on the side of the head. Poke the end of a paintbrush into each ear to both add definition and to push it securely on to the head.

9. Place the cake and the mouse in position on the plate or cake board. Use a dab of water to hold the mouse in place if necessary.

Tip · · · · · · · ·

To make a chocolate
chip cake, stir a handful
of chocolate chips
into the cake mixture
before baking.

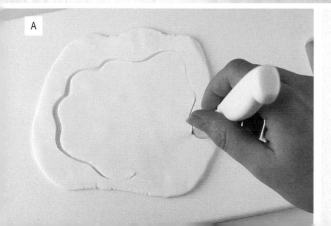

A

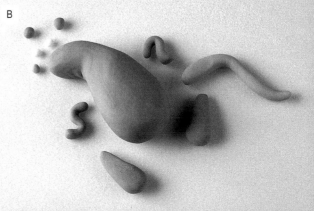

B

Chocolate Extravaganza

Deceptively easy and devilishly tasty, there really is no better cake to make for the favorite chocoholic in your life. If you're prepared for a little bit more work, you could fill the top of the cake with homemade truffles (see page 141). Either version of this cake would be ideal for Mother's Day.

INGREDIENTS
- 1 package edible decorating paper
- 5 oz. (150g) white chocolate
- 6 in. (15cm) square sponge cake (see page 13)
- 1 quantity white chocolate buttercream frosting (see page 37) or ganache (see page 137)
- Assorted chocolates

EQUIPMENT
- Scissors
- Waxed or parchment paper
- Tray
- Heatproof bowl
- Small saucepan
- Carving knife
- Palette knife
- 8 in. (20cm) square cake board
- 1 yd. (1m) ribbon

TECHNIQUES
- Melting chocolate (see page 136)
- Chocolate shapes (see page 140)
- Filling the cake (see page 38)
- Covering with buttercream (see page 38)

1. Cut the edible decorating paper into 24 rectangles about 1½ in. (4 x 8cm). They must stand higher than the edge of the cake. Place some waxed or parchment paper on a tray.

2. Melt the white chocolate. Dip the smooth side of a rectangle shape into the chocolate (see Fig. a on page 155). Place on the tray.

3. Coat four or five rectangles and then, holding both edges of the tray, bang it on your work surface a couple of times to dislodge any air bubbles. Repeat this procedure until all the rectangles have been covered. Let set.

4. To prepare the cake, level the top and turn it upside down. Slice into two or three layers and reassemble, filling the layers with buttercream frosting or ganache.

5. Spread frosting or ganache over the sides and top of the cake.

6. Peel the paper backing off the strips (Fig. a). Since it is edible, you can leave it on if you find it too difficult to peel off.

7. Press the white chocolate strips around the sides of the cake, overlapping them as you go (Fig. b).

8. Fill the top with chocolates and gently tie a bow around the outside of the cake.

Variation

Fill the top of the cake with roses for an elegant, luxurious presentation. Before placing the roses on the cake, wash the flowers and leaves with cold water then dry thoroughly.

White Chocolate Ring

Chocolate leaves are extremely simple to make and give a humble chocolate cake a lavish new look. You can use a mixture of dark, milk, and white chocolate leaves if you wish.

INGREDIENTS
- 3½ oz. (100g) white chocolate
- 7 in. (18cm) round sponge cake (see page 13)
- 1 quantity chocolate buttercream frosting (see page 37) or chocolate ganache (see page 137)

EQUIPMENT
- About 25 rose leaves
- Paper towels
- Waxed or parchment paper
- Tray
- Heatproof bowl
- Carving knife
- Palette knife
- 9 in. (23cm) round plate or cake board

TECHNIQUES
- Melting chocolate (see page 136)
- Filling the cake (see page 38)
- Covering with buttercream (see page 38)

1. Wash the rose leaves and dry them on paper towels. Place some waxed or parchment paper on a tray. Melt the white chocolate.

2. Holding a rose leaf by its stalk, dip the underside of the leaf into the chocolate (Fig. a). Lay on the waxed or parchment paper to dry.

3. To prepare the cake, slice it horizontally and fill with chocolate buttercream frosting or ganache.

4. Place the cake on a plate or cake board and spread a thick covering of frosting or ganache over the top and sides.

5. When the chocolate is set, peel the rose leaves away from the chocolate (Fig. b).

6. Gently press the leaves in a ring formation around the cake.

• •

Tip If you want to add a bit of color, lay a few rosebuds around the edge of the plate.

Variation • • • • • • • •

Construct this cake in exactly the same way, except place leaves over the top as well. Sprinkle the whole cake with a little cocoa powder, passed through a fine mesh strainer. You can make milk and semisweet chocolate leaves as well if you wish.

Choc 'n' Nut

Beware of this cake! It may be small, but it is incredibly rich and gorgeous. The use of store-bought hazelnut spread as a cake covering saves time. However, if you don't like nuts, you can use chocolate buttercream frosting or ganache, smothered with chocolate chips or crispy rice cereal instead.

INGREDIENTS
- 6 in. (15cm) round sponge cake (see page 13)
- 2 large jars chocolate hazelnut spread
- ¾ cup (95g) chopped nuts, such as walnuts or hazelnuts
- 3 oz. (90g) golden marzipan
- Cocoa powder
- Black food coloring or black food-coloring pen
- 1 whole unshelled nut, such as a pecan or hazelnut

EQUIPMENT
- Carving knife
- Palette knife
- 8 in. (20cm) round cake board
- Small sharp knife
- Fine paintbrush

TECHNIQUES
- Filling the cake (see page 38)
- Covering with buttercream (see page 38)
- Modeling with marzipan (see page 104)

Tip

Before covering the sides of the cake with the nuts, fold a sheet of waxed paper in half. Open the paper up and stand the cake on top. When finished, remove the cake, lift the paper up, fold it in half, again and pour the excess nuts either on the cake or back into the package or a plastic bag.

1. Level the top of the cake and slice the cake horizontally into two or three layers. Reassemble the cake, sandwiching it together with hazelnut spread. Place the cake on the cake board.

2. Coat the top and sides of the cake liberally with the spread. Cover the exposed cake board, too.

3. Carefully press handfuls of chopped nuts into the sides of the cake (Fig. a). You will get messy!

4. Put about ½ oz. (15g) of the marzipan aside for making the tail. Knead about 1 tsp. of cocoa powder into the rest to turn it a dark brown color.

5. Make a 1 oz. (30g) conical shape for the squirrel's body. Bend the pointed end forward slightly to make the head. Press a line into the head with a knife to make a mouth (Fig. b).

6. Make a ⅓ oz. (10g) chunky sausage shape for a leg. Squash one end to make the thigh and stick against the squirrel's body with a dab of water. Repeat on the other side with the second leg.

7. Make two tiny sausage shapes for the arms. Stick onto the squirrel's body. Position a nut in front of his tummy and place his arms onto the nut so that it looks as if the squirrel's holding it.

8. Make two triangles for the ears and stick onto the head. Add two black dots of food coloring for the eyes.

9. Roll the leftover marzipan into a flattish oval. Bend into an "S" shape and stick onto the back. Press a few lines into the tail with the back of a knife.

10. Place the squirrel onto the center of the cake and sprinkle a few nuts around him.

A

B

SUBSTITUTIONS

Some ingredients in this book may be a little difficult to find in stores. They can always be bought from an online retailer, but sometimes it may be easier or more cost-effective to make your own at home.

Candied cherries This recipe yields one cup of candied cherries. Drain a 16 oz. jar of maraschino cherries until you have ¼ cup of syrup left. Combine the syrup and sugar in a small saucepan over medium heat. Stir until all sugar crystals are dissolved. Add the cherries and stir. Bring the mixture to a boil. Cover, reduce the heat to low, and simmer for 50 to 60 minutes, or until the cherries are hard and shriveled. Remove from heat and allow the mixture to cool in the pan. Use a slotted spoon to move the cherries to a paper towel lined plate. Discard syrup. Store leftovers in an airtight container for up to six months.

Caster sugar This item can either be substituted with superfine sugar or made from granulated sugar. To do the latter, simply put the granulated sugar into a blender or food processor for a few quick pulses. The consistency should be similar to sand. Take care to not over-blend the sugar, as you will run the risk of making it too fine.

Mixed spice Combine 1 tablespoon of ground allspice, 1 tablespoon of ground nutmeg, 1 tablespoon of ground cinnamon, 2 teaspoons of ground mace, 1 teaspoon of ground cloves, 1 teaspoon of ground coriander, and 1 teaspoon of ground ginger. Store in an airtight container away from light.

SUPPLIERS

Cake & Craft
www.fondantsource.com
Offers a full selection of cake decorating supplies.

Cake Central
www.cakecentral.com
A print and online cake community for cake decorating professionals and enthusiasts.

Etsy
www.etsy.com
A global online buyer and seller community that focuses on handcrafted goods, including cake decorating.

Flour Confections
www.flourconfections.com
A Canadian company that offers a wide variety of cake decorating supplies and bakeware.

Global Sugar Art
www.globalsugarart.com
Features products for the novice to the expert cake decorator; provides tutorials and videos for select products and product reviews supplied by customers.

Inkedibles
www.inkedibles.com
A manufacturer of edible ink, edible paper, edible paints, and other edible decorations; also a supplier of chocolate making and chocolate transfer products.

The International Sugar Art Collection
www.nicholaslodge.com
Offers classes that teach all aspects of cake decorating; manufactures and distributes specialized tools and equipment.

Michaels
www.michaels.com
An arts and crafts retail chain that operates stores across the United States and Canada; offers a range of cake decorating supplies and tools.

N.Y. Cake
www.nycake.com
A retail and online company that features a variety of products, ranging from simple utensils to difficult-to-find cake tools.

Sur la Table
www.surlatable.com
With more than 100 stores, this retail company offers a selection of baking tools and supplies, including cake boards, precut paper cake liners, and specialty pans.

Wilton
www.wilton.com
Founded in 1929, Wilton built its reputation around its cake decorating and bakeware products; its website features recipes, decorating ideas, and class offerings.

To contact Carol Deacon or for further information on her books, visit her website at *www.caroldeacon.com.*

INDEX